NORTHERN ROADS

ADVANCE PRAISE

Jeremy Norton is a storyteller, and what a story he has to tell. Having pastored in the north myself for many years, I know that leadership in the far north is not for the faint of heart. My interest is how that the leadership lessons tested in the extreme circumstances of the north are of value to all of us working in less demanding contexts. Come for the stories. Leave with the insights, and you won't be disappointed.

KENTON C. ANDERSON, PHD.
President of Providence University College and Theological Seminary;
author of *Integrative Preaching* (Baker Academic)

If you feel the allure of the northern lights, value the church, and enjoy considering how the gospel and culture interact, then *Northern Roads* is a book you should be reading. Based upon his love for all things Northern, pastor and author Jeremy Norton merges his own call to ministry with unique stories of leading a church in the vast Yukon territory. In so doing, Jeremy interacts with both current church leadership philosophies and the secular trends of Canadian culture. Whether you simply like an interesting tale or prefer to take time to contemplate how to apply Christian truth to your own micro-culture, this is a book you would appreciate.

DAVID HORITA
Regional Director
Fellowship Pacific

Can a southern boy grow into a Northern man with a fruitful ministry? Evidently the answer is yes as we follow his journey through small northern communities into blessing and insights for others whether north or south. With insight into "outside the wall" ministry to team building and mentoring,

Jeremy has interesting and helpful insights into ministry beyond the geographic area he has served.

REV. DOUG BLAIR

Chair, Fellowship National Council (www.fellowship.ca)

A JOURNEY OF LIFE AND LEADERSHIP
SERVING ON THE 60TH PARALLEL

NORTHERN ROADS

JEREMY NORTON

AMBASSADOR INTERNATIONAL
GREENVILLE, SOUTH CAROLINA & BELFAST, NORTHERN IRELAND

www.ambassador-international.com

Northern Roads

A Journey of Life and Leadership Serving on the 60th Parallel
©2022 by Jeremy Norton

ISBN: 978-1-64960-128-5
eISBN: 978-1-64960-178-0

Cover Design by Hannah Linder Designs
Author photo by Narrow Road Productions
Interior Typesetting by Dentelle Design
Edited by Katie Cruice Smith

AMBASSADOR INTERNATIONAL
Emerald House
411 University Ridge, Suite B14
Greenville, SC 29601
United States
www.ambassador-international.com

AMBASSADOR BOOKS
The Mount
2 Woodstock Link
Belfast, BT6 8DD
Northern Ireland, United Kingdom
www.ambassadormedia.co.uk

The colophon is a trademark of Ambassador, a Christian publishing company.

To the pastors and church leaders who continue to spread the Gospel throughout Alaska and the Yukon.

TABLE OF CONTENTS

GOD HAS A PLAN

Have you ever contemplated whether or not our plans are really *our* plans? For me, whenever I make a sizeable decision, I wonder if God is leading that choice in some specific way. Is His distinct guidance being given through an extraordinary process? Is He coordinating certain events to achieve some greater plan that has yet to be revealed?

As I look back on my life, I have to admit that some of my decisions seemed to have been of my design. And yet, as the events unfolded, these decisions were, in fact, pivotal to a greater purpose. Not until time had passed and I was able to look back, did I see the coincidental—or what I now believe to be Providential—aspects of those decisions.

Nothing has solidified this concept more for me than the unfolding of a ministry term in Alaska that would eventually lead to a permanent calling to the Yukon Territory of Canada. At the time, it seemed like I was just accepting a unique opportunity. I had no idea that it would become the most formative years of my life or that God would use this experience to transform my calling and my future in ministry. God had a plan all along.

This book is an unpacking of the many lessons I learned during those formative years and my subsequent years of ministry in the North. These are accounts of challenge and growth, both personally and within pastoral leadership. I experienced some of the highest highs and lowest lows to date while serving in the North.

Whether you've picked up this book because of the Northern content or the ministry content, I assure you that both are equally as vast and wild.

My prayer is that the journey found within these pages will help guide your ministry in some way and that you might learn and grow as I did. So, here's my Northern Roads story—a journey of life and leadership serving on the 60th parallel.

PART ONE

CALLED TO THE NORTH

CHAPTER ONE

WHEN COINCIDENTAL PROVIDENCE STRIKES

"Many are the plans in the mind of a man,
but it is the purpose of the LORD that will stand."

Proverbs 19:21

My wife, Nicole, and I were living in Airdrie, Alberta, Canada. At that time, Airdrie was a relatively small, bedroom community that fed the large urban center of Calgary. Every morning seemed to come fast and furious during those days. The alarm clock went off, and I was on my feet out of necessity, not out of the enjoyment of a new day. I would shower and shave, iron my shirt, eat a quick bite, and head out the door. My vehicle joined the endless stream of commuters on Highway 2, also known as the Deerfoot Trail, headed into the city.

I had a full-time sales position within the hospitality industry. It was a good job, and I was experiencing relative success, meeting sales targets and receiving bonuses. That being said, having a salary-plus-bonus pay structure meant the hours tended to be quite long. Nicole was pregnant with our first child, due in a little over a month. There were signs that the baby might come early, so her doctor had put her on bedrest soon into the third trimester. There was a looming nervousness that the baby could come at any moment. Nicole followed the doctor's orders and focused on giving her body (and our baby) the rest they needed.

As if this pace of life was not stressful enough, I was also doing night classes at Alberta Bible College to finish my degree. The hope was to move into full-time ministry as soon as possible. As I think back now, this was an exhausting time in my life. And yet, the goal of a ministry career was in the distance. God's calling carried me forward through each tumultuous day. When I was only a few courses away from completing my degree, it was time to start putting my resume out there. I went straight to Google and found a variety of Christian and ministry-focused job sites. I opened the first search result and started to complete the required online profile. I filled in the typical fields: Personal Information, Education, Employment History, etc.

Then I reached a field asking for my desired work location, represented by a drop-down menu of countries, states, provinces, and territories. At the time, I had my preferences, but I was just thankful to be moving into full-time ministry. I needed some experience, and I believed that God was sovereign over the process. So, I clicked every province and territory throughout Canada. Then I came upon an option to relocate to another country. I hovered over the United States. I didn't want to move to the States, but Nicole was American. I decided that I owed it to her to at least click her home state of Alaska. Then I moved on with the rest of the form. After that, I continued to make this token Alaskan selection for each website. What were the chances that a church in Alaska would want me?

THE CLICK THAT ALTERED MY FUTURE

A couple of weeks later, I received a call from a senior pastor named Keith. He asked if I would like to candidate for their youth pastor position. As he gave his initial pitch, he noted that the church was located in—would you believe it—Alaska! My mind was swimming as Pastor Keith gave his overview of the church and location. He explained that the church was located in Soldotna, Alaska. I couldn't believe it. Everything went into slow motion— first, disbelief, and then speculation started to take root.

Alaska is the largest state in the U.S., yet this church was only half an hour from Nicole's hometown. I was certain that there had to be more going on behind the scenes. *This is happening too quickly!* I thought. *This can't be where God wants me to serve!* (Enter my pride and lack of faith.) Then it came to me; my mother-in-law must have intervened! It made total sense. Nicole's mother, Diane, worked as a church secretary for a church in the next town over. *She's working some angle to get us into Alaska.* We were just about to have a new baby, and she'd love to get her hands on him. This gave her plenty of motive to intervene. Diane likely heard through Nicole that there was a slim chance that I was willing to move to Alaska. Then she started calling some church connections.

Meanwhile, Keith was waiting for my response. And I was preparing to decline. After all, if I was going to accept a ministry position, it was going to be the work of God's sovereign hand, not my mother-in-law's intervention. But before I made my decision, I wanted to confirm my suspicions.

"You must have received my name and number from my mother-in-law?" My tone was holding a sense of question and statement at the same time.

"How would I know your mother-in-law?" Keith asked, clearly indicating his bewilderment.

I explained with confidence, "Well, my wife grew up in Nikiski. My mother-in-law, Diane, works for a church not far from you in Kenai. I assume she gave you my name and number as a potential candidate."

With great enthusiasm, Keith said, "Your wife grew up in Nikiski? Have you ever been up here?"

"A couple of times," I replied.

"So, you've been to Soldotna, Alaska?"

"Yeah, I'm almost certain you pass right through Soldotna to get to my in-laws' house," I answered.

"Do you know how hard it is to find an American who knows where Soldotna is, never mind a Canadian?" Keith exclaimed with excitement.

All of a sudden, the hair on the back of my neck stood up, and I was drenched in shame.

"Where did you get my name and number?" I tried to keep a jovial tone, though feeling quite foolish.

Keith replied, "Our admin assistant found you on YouthPastor.com a few days ago and passed on the info. I browsed through your profile and decided it'd be worth giving you a call."

As you've likely guessed, I accepted his request to candidate. As I hung up the phone, my head continued to spin. Nicole called her mother right away to tell her that I would be candidating for a church in Alaska. Her parents were elated by the news. Unfortunately, my speculative outlook on the situation prevented me from fully sharing in their joy. I was still ashamed. How blinded was I with my pride? It amazes me how quickly sin can steal the obvious conclusions from our minds. My arrogance had prevented me from enjoying that incredible moment. My pride had stolen the bliss of God's sovereignty. The whole experience could have been so different. My selfishness and ego stole the joy that my wife and in-laws were reveling in.

Pride doesn't die easily, though, does it? Believe it or not, I had the nerve to ask Diane if she had spoken to the pastor. That's right! Just when you thought my arrogant heart had given up, it stepped back in again. This time, I was convinced that my mother-in-law had spoken to Pastor Keith but that they had worked out this plan that he had found my name on the internet. I know—who thinks like that? And how could I ever think that I was ready for a ministry career with that kind of heart condition? The Lord had some major heart surgery to do in the years ahead.

Only a week or two prior, I had made a single click beside one of the fifty states listed under the United States form at YouthPastor.com. Lo and behold, a week later, a church in Alaska visited the same website, looking for someone to relocate to their Northern location. There was no angle, no conversations, no ulterior motives. Just God doing what God does. Our Heavenly Father making sure that His plan prevails regardless of my inability to trust in His ability. Something unique was beginning to unfold. God was writing me into an incredible story. I didn't realize it at the time, but He was laying out a plan that would carry massive significance for my future. Looking back, I can see how that single click began a ministry journey specifically designed for me. Some Northern town needed me. More importantly, I would come to find out that I needed that Northern town.

THE EMBARRASSING TRUTH

It's embarrassing to type the words found in this first chapter. To recount that series of events. My pride had prevented me from seeing how diverse and multi-layered God's sovereign hand can weave a plan for His purposes. But that's where I was. And I don't believe that I'm the only one who's ever been there. There have to be others who have shown the same lack of faith. There have to be others who have allowed pride and arrogance to steal the delight of God's provision.

When we first start in ministry, we're passionate enough, that's for sure. But there's also a haughtiness that can take over, convincing us that we have all the answers. We start to believe that everyone is wrong or working some sort of angle. We make it our mission to get to the bottom of it. It's faithless, thinking that God can't or won't overcome these petty circumstances of life. His will and plan will prevail, even if our sin prevents the elation of that experience. King Solomon's proverbial wisdom holds great truth in that: "The heart of man plans his way, but the LORD establishes his steps" (Prov. 16:9).

God has a plan, and we've been invited into it. For whatever reason, sometimes it's hard for us to remember that fact. Sure, the plan might be challenging. It might mean that areas of sin and insecurity are brought to the forefront. Possibly, even exposed! It will likely mean learning lessons in patience and endurance. It might also mean that the comfortable areas of our lives will be taken from us. On the flipside, we might be carried into an unforeseen journey to a place that we never envisioned being. In truth, we can probably count on all of that taking place. But it'll be okay. We can trust Him. He has a way of showing us that the apparent coincidence is often His providence.

Within a week or so, an official telephone interview took place with the church's search committee. It went very well. Immediately following that interview, plans for a candidate trip were set into motion. Nicole and I, along with our new baby boy, would head up for a weekend visit to Alaska. As excitement and nervousness grew, a hint of humility finally started to pierce my heart. Nicole and I shared in prayers of thanksgiving. We could hardly believe what had transpired in such a short time.

We flew up to Alaska to candidate over a single weekend. The trip was quite a blur, but everything went as planned. I was able to meet many of the students and their families. We toured around the area, talking about where we would live if we accepted the position. Then we went into a congregational meeting, where I fielded several questions on an array of topics. Before we knew it, the weekend was over, and we were on a plane back to Canada.

A few days later, I received another phone call from Pastor Keith. This time, he offered me the position. Of course, by this time, I had completely resolved to the fact that through a unique set of circumstances, I was going to be living and serving in Alaska. I had accepted the position to get us moved as soon as possible. Easy enough, right? Not exactly.

It turned out that getting a Canadian into the United States wasn't as simple as one would think—especially if you're trying to do everything by the book. For a small, Alaskan church without significant access or resources for immigration attorneys, hiring me proved to be quite a challenge. The congregation was ready to have us. I was ready to serve. And Nicole's family was desperate for us to move. We were ready to go! But would the United States government take us?

Mentally, I had submitted to the extraordinary circumstances surrounding this call. I had answered this call and was committed to serving in Alaska. One would think that this immigration component would easily be taken care of by God. Surely, the Lord would intervene to keep this ball rolling. That's not what happened, though. It ended up being a huge lead-up, followed by a hurry-up, and then a wait.

WAITING IS DIFFICULT

Waiting is so difficult. When you're waiting, there are a dozen different scenarios that play out in your mind. It tests your ability to be patient. Then it often leads to struggles of doubt. Patience and doubt work like a tag-team on your mind when you're in a season of waiting. *Is this God's plan? Is this roadblock a warning to find a different path?*

Needless to say, the coming months were difficult—heading into work, day in and day out, knowing that I would be leaving but not knowing when I could hand in my resignation. We worked with the church, seeking immigration counsel and getting paperwork in order. In the meantime, phone conversations with family held a lot of rhetorically prayerful questions like, "What's the hold-up, Lord?" So many questions surfaced. Even though, in the back of our minds, we knew the waiting was good for us. We were learning patience and endurance, but we didn't want to.

Think about the last time a friend or family member was in a season of waiting. We're often the ones encouraging them, reminding them of God's faithfulness, explaining to them, how the waiting teaches us patience and endurance. We don't think like that when we're the ones waiting, though, do we? For some reason, it's difficult for us to self-talk ourselves into being patient and enduring.

Then it finally happened! Thanks be to God, after four months of waiting, I was finally approved for entry. As a pastor, I was granted an R1 or religious worker permit. This R1 status would give me three years of service before I would have to return to Canada. Alternately, at the end of three years, there would be an option for the church to apply for a two-year extension. This could result in a total five-year term. That was the plan.

With our permit in hand and all of our belongings loaded into the moving truck, we began our twenty-two-hundred-mile journey from Airdrie, Alberta, northwest to the Kenai Peninsula of Alaska. We rolled out, turning north onto Highway 2 toward Edmonton, then soon were heading west. At Dawson Creek, we officially started the Alaska Highway. From there, we followed the ALCAN route into British Columbia, then into the Yukon Territory and through "The Wilderness City" of Whitehorse, which would eventually be the location of our permanent calling in the years to come.

When we reached the border at Beaver Creek, Yukon, I was nervous. I had heard some terrible stories of border guards conducting thorough searches, which could mean pulling apart belongings and leaving the mess beside the vehicle for the owners to handle. We had done some research to prevent this from happening. As per the instructions we found, we had created a detailed manifest of every piece of cargo. We wrote a number on every box that matched a content list on the manifest. The hope was the border guards would search a few random boxes, checking to see if it matched the manifest, and be satisfied.

It turned out that we did a lot of work for nothing. There were a couple of easy questions and a quick look at my R1 permit, returning it to me with a hardy, "Welcome to the United States!"

Really? That's it? I thought momentarily. But that was immediately followed by, *Who cares? We're on our way!*

We rolled into Alaska, but we were far from finished with our journey. Alaska is the biggest state in the U.S., and the border was nowhere near our destination. We still had another eighteen hours of driving to get down to the Kenai Peninsula. As we drove, we were filled with wonder, not only at the incredible creation that the Last Frontier holds, but also at how God's hand had been evident throughout the entire relocation process. God had been faithful. His plan had been revealed. Crossing that border was the final confirmation of this unexpected call to serve in the North.

CHAPTER TWO

NATIONAL PRIDE CAN COME BEFORE A FALL

"Do not love the world or the things in the world. If anyone loves the world,
the love of the Father is not in him. For all that is in the world—
the desires of the flesh and the desires of the eyes and pride of life—
is not from the Father but is from the world."

1 John 2:15-16

Small-town Alaska was more of an adjustment than I had anticipated. In a big city, there's often a diversity of cultures. Even neighborhood to neighborhood, age or income levels can shift the culture of a particular district. Small-town culture has a completely different make-up. Small towns can be difficult to navigate if you've never lived in one. Because of the lower population, the entire town often takes on the culture of the majority, which spreads quite easily.

This is a culture that has been established over many years and will not easily change. Those who want to buck the culture of their small town usually have to leave and settle elsewhere. Time spent there often proves one's value in a small town. A newcomer with a new idea will not be accepted in the same way that a long-standing resident might be. The same idea presented by someone who has been established in the culture over many years may find immediate community support. I soon found out that small, Northern towns held all of these cultural distinctives and intricacies.

Before I continue, consider the fact that I was new to the country, new to the state, and new to the community. That meant I was about to get schooled big time! I was way out of my comfort zone. I would have to gain a cultural understanding of the United States, Alaska, and the Kenai Peninsula. Moreover, there's also an array of Northern-living cultural nuances weaved into societal dynamics that were completely foreign to me. I would need to be humble, listening to and learning everything, so that I could integrate into and serve this community. Unfortunately, I didn't do that.

I was way too arrogant for that. In truth, America and I had a bit of history. More than just marrying an American, that is. This history filled me with assumptions that came rushing to the surface in a whirlwind of pride and insecurity. This history would make my first year in small-town Alaska incredibly difficult. The Lord would allow me to walk through this difficult season so that I might gain a rich knowledge and appreciation not just for Alaskans, but for the United States as a whole. Before we get there, allow me to unpack the history that America and I have.

LIVING NEAR AMERICANS

Like many Canadians, I'm proud to be from the "True North strong and free." However, in years past, my national pride had become a stumbling block and hurtful to many American friends and colleagues. Now that I have somewhat matured, I can look back and see where my struggles began. I can see how a lot of it was based on my insecurities.

I grew up in Sarnia, Ontario, a small city of seventy-three thousand bordering Port Huron, Michigan. To anyone who has ever lived in a community like this, you'll understand the unique relationship that develops with the people on the *other* side of the border. It's like a competition, but typically only one side is accepting (or even aware of) the challenge.

Canadian border towns experience this unique phenomenon quite often. On one hand, we love living on the U.S. border, enjoying American stores and restaurants. For me, bordering Southern Michigan meant heading down to Detroit on weekends to check out major sporting events and concerts. For most Canadians, we crave and devour everything that America has to offer. Some have even argued that we need America socially, financially, militarily, etc. All of this irritates us, for some reason.

Instead of being thankful for our neighbors, it seems like we resent them. Maybe it's because we do need them. Maybe neighboring the United States is a blessing that we take for granted. Truth be told, inside many Canadian hearts, there's a strange competition raging, but we've never invited Americans to the tournament. They're often oblivious. If we're not careful, soon the pride we have for our nation can become an internal arrogance. That was my problem. On the outside, I loved everyone and everything that was America. But internally, I had fully bought into the mentality that as a Canadian, I'm on some sort of higher social status. I was better than them somehow. I was so lost and so arrogant.

Then I met an American who broke every stereotype that any Canadian has ever heard or created. By the time I got into my first year of college, I managed to hide my hurtful thoughts about Americans. So much so, I actually agreed to having an American roommate from Buffalo, New York. For the most part, I pulled off the con that year. It would end up progressing, though, as all sinful things do. I was shifty. I would save my opinions for when the Americans weren't around. Then I was just downright hurtful.

It was during that first year of college that it happened. God gave His first impactful blow against my arrogant heart. This blow would be a vital piece to His purposed plan for my life and ministry. I fell in love with an American.

She was a quiet girl from a small town in Alaska. For the first part of the school year, I had ignored her. Not her fault. I was an extreme extrovert and naturally navigated toward high energy and volume. She was neither of these. Then late one night in the library, I realized that we were the only two people there. I decided to start up a conversation with her, which I didn't think would last more than five minutes. But that five minutes turned into hours! This shy, wallflower, Northern girl captivated me.

She described a simple life that was completely foreign to how and where I grew up. Fishing and hunting for subsistence to keep the freezer full of meat, instead of for hobby or sport. Her dad had a pick-up truck in the driveway out front and a floatplane on the lake out back. Before college, she was a member of the high school ski team. She loved winter and snow. The moose was her favorite animal, and in her opinion, the cutest. She was graceful and grounded, with a meek femininity equaled only by her independent resolve. More importantly, she was sold out for Jesus with unwavering faith in Him. She was amazing, and I was smitten.

Meeting Nicole, now my wife of twenty years, would be the first step in breaking down my sinful pride—a pride that was so carefully disguised as national pride. God had a purpose for my life, and He knew what was needed to get me on track. In time, we would be blessed with three incredible sons, who hold both Canadian and American passports. And considering their mother is American, maybe one of them could be president one day? Republican or Democrat? Great question, and a great segue.

AREN'T ALL CHRISTIANS REPUBLICANS?

I'll never forget the first time I heard the assumption that all Christians vote Republican. It was during the candidate trip. Trying to get a feel for the culture early on, I listened to a lot of local talk radio during that trip. I discovered that there was a lot of political banter, specifically concerning the federal election, which was still six months away. At the time, I was surprised. Yet I would come to find out that this is typical in the United States. Political reporting this far in advance is an expected piece of American politics, priming the pump for the main event. At that time, President Bush would soon complete his presidency. The McCain versus Obama race was on, and it was heated! Both parties were extremely confident in their candidates.

During the candidate trip, we would visit a few homes for dinner to get to know some of the congregation. One of these evenings was spent with a family whose oldest son would soon be in the youth ministry. The parents had a vested interest in who I was and what I was all about. Both parents were well-educated, with prominent positions in our local community. As well as having their son in our youth group, they would become valuable ministry partners. I was looking forward to getting to know them better.

Before dinner, we were chit-chatting a bit about church philosophy and possible ministry plans if I were to take the position. All discussions with no real agenda, other than just getting to know one another better. During a lull in the conversation, I tried to make some small talk. I remembered the talk radio banter.

"How do you think most people around here will vote in the election?" I asked.

He looked at me as if I had just flown in from Mars.

"We're in Alaska!" he remarked.

Seeing that I didn't get his obvious hint, he went on to explain that most people in Alaska are very conservative, especially on the Kenai Peninsula. Therefore, almost everyone votes Republican. As we continued our discussion, he explained how the majority of evangelical Christians in the United States typically vote Republican. This was interesting to me since, in any given Canadian church, it's a toss-up in trying to guess who's voting for whom. This was not the case in the United States. I would soon find out that this gentlemen's claim was fairly accurate. At least, at that moment in history. (The future election between Presidents Trump and Biden would prove that communication style and character can carry as much weight as policies and platform.) Nevertheless, though not often stated directly but often implied at that time was the fact that to be Christian was to vote Republican.

What does that mean for Christians who vote Democrat? I wondered.

Months later, when my paperwork was in order and upon permanent arrival to the Kenai Peninsula, I got into a routine fairly quickly—up early and heading down to the local coffee shop. Within those first few weeks, there was a serious buzz in the air regarding the upcoming election. As I listened and took part in conversations, I struggled to understand the cultural hype behind these two political juggernaut parties of Republican and Democrat. There were flickers of fire for Independent and Libertarian parties, but I never saw any news coverage on these parties or their candidates. It became clear that these two governing giants were fundamentally, and indefinitely, destined to face off against each other. They would be ready to do political battle every four years, no matter what. Little did I know that this was an important piece of information for me to understand. To grasp American culture, one must grasp its political system. Including the long-standing history of back and forth, Democrat-Republican, Republican-Democrat, party-to-party, win, reign, loss, and re-gain. It seems to have been and has continued to be, a never-ending struggle.

At that time, as a Canadian, I felt so separated from this society where politics played such an integral part of daily life. Back home, politics always seemed like a practical or mechanical entity. Don't get me wrong. Canadians care about political outcomes, but not to this extent. Furthermore, and coming back to the Christian perspective, with every coffee shop conversation came the same underlying message that I had heard four months previously. I was getting the message that a true Alaskan ought not to vote for a donkey. Moreover, as I met with Christians in the community and listened to church foyer banter, the opinion was made clear that to follow Jesus meant voting Republican.

This was difficult for me to understand in the beginning. My personal experience and biblical conviction had caused me to believe that Jesus didn't care too much about politics at all. Nevertheless, I was about to learn that many of my brothers and sisters in Christ, serving equally as His bride, held some varying opinions regarding Christ's view of politics in general. In the next few years, I would come to understand the diversity of issues and cultural impacts that politics play in conservative, evangelical America. My opinions would shift the more I understood. But in those first few months, I was very confused.

DO I BELONG HERE?

It was during those early conversations regarding how a Christian should vote that I started to get nervous. Even though I didn't hold the right to vote because of my status in the United States, I still sensed an underlying pressure to promote Republican values, not just as a Christian but also as a pastor. Gradually, I could feel my back against the wall as my insecurity grew. Once again, my heart was being pulled away from what I was called to do—serving Jesus and serving this community.

What am I doing here? I would ask myself. *How can I pastor anyone with all of this pressure? Surely, I'm not the right guy for the job. Maybe I should just quit and go home!*

If you can believe it, within those first few months, I would debate the pros and cons of quitting several times. Rightly or wrongly, I always came to the same conclusion.

"Nicole would be devastated. Suck it up and deal with it."

In hindsight, I should have relied on Christ's strength and refocused my thoughts on the situation. But that's not what happened. I didn't rely on Christ's strength, and I didn't refocus my thoughts. Instead, it was in those first few months that my long-standing struggle started to rear its ugly head again. And it would continue to be a struggle for the coming months. I could feel that old resentment from my teenage years creeping back. I started embracing the emotional responses of that sixteen-year-old border town kid, who I thought had disappeared a long time ago. My sin was giving me a great excuse, as sin always does.

In my mind, I constantly pointed to the pressure that I was feeling to teach teens what was right, which I felt included Republican values. But if I had been thinking clearly, I would have seen the numerous lessons and opportunities. Those conversations were unique touch-points for growth. Moreover, I would have heard my senior pastor, Keith, supporting my ministry wholeheartedly. His desire and his advice to me were to disregard external pressure and focus on the ministry to which God had called me. Unfortunately, I just didn't pay attention to his encouragement. I lost my focus entirely.

Men's Breakfast was a big eye-opener into conservative American and Alaskan culture. Once a month, the men would gather at the church for breakfast. We'd have a devotional thought or sometimes watch a Christian hunting video. Following breakfast, we'd occasionally go out to a work project for someone in the church or community. It was a fairly relaxed environment to catch up with the guys without the hustle and bustle of Sunday morning chit-chat. Every once in a while, we would host the ever-popular "Pistols & Pancakes!" Americana at its finest! The guys would go out shooting after their hearty breakfast. It might seem odd to some, but it was a great entry point for Alaskan men to experience the Church.

Men's Breakfast was one of the few adult ministry environments that worked for my schedule as the youth pastor. Looking back, it would end up becoming one of my favorites. To this day, I miss it a lot, even though my first few Men's Breakfasts were not so comfortable.

As I explained earlier, I was already feeling a heightened insecurity and pressure from cultural differences. All of this wrapped itself up in an uneasy feeling that I didn't quite fit in with the rest of the guys. I'll never forget my very first Men's Breakfast in October of 2008. I had only been in the state for a month. Like everywhere else, the upcoming election was the main topic of conversation. Over breakfast, many of the men explained their anger at the Liberal attack ads, where Democrats worked hard to highlight every error that President Bush had made during his terms. They discussed recent news segments, where Liberals were throwing out a barrage of hateful titles like "imbecile" and "warmonger," adding that the opposing Left was planting the opinion that by electing John McCain, the country would result in the same kind of leadership. There was a serious tone in the room as the men discussed the future of their country.

The next month flew by, and the November Men's Breakfast rolled around a few days after the 2008 presidential election. The Democrats had won, and for the first time, the United States had elected an African American president, Barack Obama. Not just a minority in the ethnic sense, but also from lower social status, born to a foreign father, who had left him to be raised by his single American mother. This was a very different president than the country was used to having as their leader. And yet, what would seem like a win against the political elite would not be celebrated around our breakfast table.

To be sure, there was a chill in the air that morning, and it wasn't just from the weather. The men looked like they had just lost their jobs, their homes, and their families, all in one shot. Sure, their side had lost the election, but these men looked truly defeated. I was so confused.

As we shuffled to the tables with our man-grub in hand, the conversations began. The men were so angry and looked as though they were legitimately hurting inside. This would be a safe environment for them to share their frustrations with the country's drastic shift in leadership. I listened as the men shared their concern for their future, not just as a nation, but as individuals. They firmly believed that their livelihoods and values were about to be taken away. They were devastated!

ALL THINGS TO ALL PEOPLE

Once again, I marveled at how closely related politics was to an individual's well-being. Only two months into my position, it was yet another wake-up call that understanding American and Alaskan culture may be my greatest challenge to ministering here. When we enter into a new culture or environment, we need to rely on Christ's strength to engage the people. The lies that come with insecurity will tell us that we're not good enough or that we're not the right person for the job. We'll shy away from tough conversations and pretend everything's fine. In my case, pressures related to cultural differences would bring about unresolved sin that I had been ignoring for years. Over time, God began to open my eyes, reminding me, "No temptation has overtaken you that is not common to man. God is faithful, and he will not let you be tempted beyond your ability, but with the temptation he will also provide the way of escape, that you may be able to endure it" (1 Cor. 10:13).

God would gradually show me that by accepting His call to serve this American-Alaskan community, it would mean taking some serious steps toward understanding them, engaging in their values, and adapting to their way of life. Paul's call to the Corinthian church is fitting to "become all things to all people...for the sake of the gospel" (1 Cor. 9:22-23). Even if that meant entertaining conversations about—gulp— Republican Jesus or Democrat Jesus, for that matter. The ability to bridge the relationship gap for deeper conversation was worth it. I would have to swallow my pride and insecurity and at least listen to their point of view.

Obviously, those first few months were difficult, and I was struggling. Thankfully, God is faithful, reminding us that the Gospel remains primary, that everyone needs Jesus, but that there are many ways to lead someone to Him. He was faithful in the grace He showed me when I needed it. And He was steadfast in allowing me to trip and fall when I needed that. He was faithful. And soon, He would provide the help I needed to become an American, Alaskan, and Northern culture-savvy pastor.

CHAPTER THREE

AMERICA, CANADA, OR HEAVEN?

"But our citizenship is in heaven, and from it we await a Savior, the Lord Jesus Christ, who will transform our lowly body to be like his glorious body, by the power that enables him even to subject all things to himself."

Philippians 3:20-21

My first year of ministry was moving forward with fairly consistent success. It was packed with meetings, events, and projects—all of which seemed to roll along seamlessly. I had a senior pastor and an elder's board who gave me creative control over my assigned ministries and monitored progress from a distance. I managed to build a small, fairly structured team of adults, and student leaders. We were seeing small amounts of growth spiritually and in actual numbers. Life was good, or so everyone thought.

God had started to do some major work on my heart, but the internal battle waged on during that first year of ministry. Most of it centered on my insecurities and identity within American culture. I often felt lonely, even though I was surrounded by people. There were constant reminders that in this conservative Alaskan culture, I was the odd man out. It wasn't that I was embarrassed in the least about being Canadian. I just didn't seem to fit in anywhere. Though I tried to remind myself of my calling, the truth was that I thought differently, acted differently, and most notably, spoke differently.

Believe it or not, my voice became a stumbling block, putting my back up against the wall again and again. The Canadian accent is most recognizable when using words containing the vowels of *o* and *u*, followed by a consonant. If you can't picture it, find yourself a Canadian and get them to say, "Out and about." You'll hear the difference loud and clear. To get a good laugh, ask them, if they're comfortable, to say this little rhyme to recall their accent: "There's a mouse in the house; get it out, get it out."

Too often, it seemed that my accent was just a way to ease into discussing some political or cultural issues. Half of the conversations I had in my first year of ministry reminded me that although I spoke the same language, there was a massive divide between me and the people around me. I often felt out of place. These conversations were a greater struggle with family, people from church, or people in the community that I got to know on a personal level. God was testing my calling day in and day out, but I was failing miserably. I was having an internal problem but was convincing myself that it was an external one. Once again, I was neglecting to rely on Christ's strength.

As a Christian, my identity should be rooted in Christ, not in my nationality—and definitely not in the difference of accent that a nationality may hold. There was a pride and arrogance that had been established many years before. It had been so easily hidden on Canadian soil, but it was time for it to be removed. God slowly but surely continued His surgical work on my heart. I was neglecting an eternal perspective, and God knew exactly how to bring it to the forefront of my life and ministry. Thankfully, during this time of refinement, God would encourage me along the way. He would balance out His correction with His grace by bringing me a Canadian friend.

SCOTT FROM VANCOUVER

Turns out that I wasn't the only Canadian in Alaska. And I wasn't the only Canadian on the Kenai Peninsula either. I ended up meeting a few of them while I was there. For anyone who has spent an extended amount of time in another country, you will know the great joy that comes from meeting one of your countrymen. Back home, you might not have been friends, but now that you've met abroad, there's a kinship that is quite extraordinary. There is one such friend to whom I owe a great many thanks.

Scott had moved to Alaska from Vancouver, British Columbia, some years previous. He had met his bride-to-be, Kathy, on a Christian dating site. They fell in love and worked through the process to move Scott into the United States permanently. They both attended our church, so Scott and I would chat quite frequently. And chats with Scott were never superficial. Sure, there was Canadian banter, but Scott was constantly checking in to see that I was encouraged and that life was moving along well. Almost weekly, he would pull me aside, put his hand on my shoulder, look my straight in the eye, and ask, "How you doin', Man?"

This likely had no significance within typical conversations, but when he asked, he meant it. Scott cared about how I was doing. Not only did he provide quality friendship and support, but Scott and Kathy would also open their home to our family on a consistent basis. As soon as we entered, the Tim Horton's coffee was pulled out of the cupboard. As he scooped the grinds into the coffee maker, Scott would always turn to me with a grin and quote the brand slogan, "Tim Horton's, Always Fresh!"

Sometimes I wondered if I came over just to hear that little slogan. Soon enough, Canadian topics and current events were being discussed and debated. As the oldest in my family, I'm unfamiliar with what it feels like to have an older brother. I imagined that perhaps this is what it should feel like. Very early on, he became the older brother that was a safe source to explain the insecurities I was feeling within American culture. It felt like he and I were like-minded in so many ways. Scott was Canadian. He understood the differences and from where my struggles stemmed. He also helped in bridging the gap between myself and the Alaskan-American mindset that I was struggling to understand. Other than Scott, I'm not sure that anyone fully knew what I was thinking and feeling. He was pivotal to my success in Alaska, and I will never forget that.

Meanwhile, Kathy would pour herself into serving my wife and son—not only through hospitality, but also through purposeful engagement into how Nicole was doing. Their house felt like home. Over the entire ministry term in Alaska, both Scott and Kathy were great friends and a constant source of gracious support to Nicole and me. God provides these types of friendships during pivotal times in our lives, and they become lasting ones. God used these two people, and we miss them very much, still relishing visits with them whenever we can get them.

CHANGE IN PERSPECTIVE

By the end of my first year, even with Scott's support, I was feeling pretty defeated. After one year of serving and not fitting in, I started to wonder why I had come to Alaska in the first place. The loneliness of the past year had taken its toll. I was struggling to understand why God would allow me so much ministry success yet allow so much struggle in my personal life. I was ready to give it all up. Flat out, I just wanted to go home.

That was until one particular morning, almost exactly one year from arrival. That morning, I shuffled into our local coffee shop and ordered. After a bit of chit-chat with the barista, I received my coffee and sat down in the corner of the shop. As was my routine, I turned on my laptop, then opened my web-browser to BibleGateway.com, ready to have my morning devotional time with the Lord. I had been going through this routine almost daily. God often blessed me with excellent insight into life and ministry during these quiet times. In hindsight, it's likely why I didn't quit in the first few months.

Most mornings, I seemed to get enough "Bread of Life" to sustain me for the day's events. It curbed the loneliness just enough to keep me focused. However, I never really allowed God's Word to penetrate deep enough to show me what was going on deep inside my insecure heart. This morning would be very different. I was not expecting the revelation that I was about to receive that morning. Over the past couple of weeks, I had been working through the Epistles during this time. I was on track to start the book of First Peter. As I read the first chapter, I started to receive a major change in perspective.

Peter's first epistle begins with rich content pointing to God's sovereignty and mysterious salvation-work. Scriptures relating to this doctrine have always been of interest to me. So, I was locked in as I moved through the verses. Then verse thirteen hit me like a freight train. "Therefore, preparing your minds for action, and being sober-minded, set your hope fully on the grace that will be brought to you at the revelation of Jesus Christ" (1 Peter 1:13).

That was it. My entire perspective shifted. Content-wise, it was pretty straight forward and not much to unpack. But for me, in that moment, God used six words to spark a fire in my heart. "Therefore, preparing your minds for action . . . " All of a sudden, my mind was racing with a full year's worth of self-reflective thought.

"There it is! That's where I've been going wrong!"

I finally accepted that the problem wasn't the people, the community, the state, or even the country. The problem was me! After reading that passage in First Peter, I was awakened to my purpose and calling once again. For the past year I had been allowing my insecurities to lead my thought patterns. I'd been focusing on the least important factors of why I came to Alaska to begin with. It was time to fully submit to God's plan, address my sin, and prepare my mind for action. I was not going to retreat from the incredible experience into which God had placed me.

As I think back to that morning, it amazes me how badly I had lost my focus. Within my ministry, I was starting to see some tangible, concrete fruit from the discipleship into which I was investing so much time. I had a great leadership team around me, who were on board with the vision for the upcoming years of ministry. I had been neglecting the celebration of what had been accomplished. And I was lacking focus on the diverse works that still needed to be completed.

It was at that moment, almost one year after starting my position, that I finally allowed God to completely cut out the sin that I had carried for so many years. At that moment, I finally let Him take control of my heart and my ministry. Despite my personal feelings regarding the cultural landscape, I was all in, and my insecurities were out! This is where I was called. I started to fall in love with America and Americans and with Alaska and Alaskans. I would fall deeply in love with Northern life and culture. It would become a part of me that would eventually grow into something truly amazing.

FOCUSING ON ETERNAL REWARDS

After many years of growth, and now living back in Canada, I feel blessed that I understand the uniqueness of both countries. I can so easily see where most conversations break down from social, cultural, and definitely political value differences. Americans and Canadians share a continent, but they are vastly different! After living in the United States, it is so evident to me that patriotism and national pride can easily slip into sinful pride, regardless of the flag we raise. Instead, our identity can only be found in Christ and a unity of all nations that flows out of that identity. I love what Paul wrote to the church in Philippi. "But our citizenship is in heaven, and from it we await a Savior, the Lord Jesus Christ, who will transform our lowly body to be like his glorious body, by the power that enables him even to subject all things to himself. Therefore, my brothers, whom I love and long for, my joy and crown, stand firm thus in the Lord, my beloved" (Phil. 3:20-4:1).

This is what is so amazing about "set[ting our] minds on the things that are above" (Col. 3:2). Once we establish in our minds that our true citizenship is in Heaven, it can sink into our hearts. If we can picture ourselves in Heaven, united with men and women from every tribe and tongue (Rev. 7:9), it can transform who we are in our earthly lives. The only flag we raise is the banner of Christ, with a pride that is based on authentic worship of the One Who has saved all nations throughout history. This vision of things to come is our eternal reward for embracing a Christ-centred identity.

For those of us in ministry, we're likely going to cross paths with people from every walk of life, some of whom we may easily embrace over cultural understanding or even personal similarities. Others may grind on everything we believe to be right or normal. Perhaps we're in conflict with some of these cultural differences. Maybe we've been forced to choose sides over a particular issue. This has the potential to damage relationships, and if not dealt with quickly and thoroughly, it may even damage our ministry.

Before making any rash decisions, we must set our minds on the view from Heaven. Look down at the situation. Look down at the issue. Think about our future life. Think about our eternity with Christ. How important are the differences and issues from that perspective? We must remember that whomever we meet and whatever they may represent, our earthly preferences are trivial. Instead, we must choose to concentrate on our heavenly citizenship.

PART TWO

FALLING IN LOVE
WITH THE NORTH

CHAPTER FOUR

SIXTEEN-OUNCE DRIP WITH ROOM

"Jesus answered her, 'If you knew the gift of God, and who it is that is saying to you, Give me a drink, you would have asked him, and he would have given you living water.'"

John 4:10

On Alaska's Kenai Peninsula, there's a road that connects the prominent communities of Soldotna and Kenai named the Kalifornsky Beach Road. Locally, this road is simply known as K-Beach. Tucked in the middle of K-Beach is a coffee shop named Small Town Coffee Roasters. Locally known as Coffee Roasters—perhaps for obvious reasons—this place is a hub for locals. If I was going to get to know this community and understand the culture, this was the kind of place to do it.

Local shops like Coffee Roasters can become the core of community relationships. And yet the shops may look very different depending on the geographic location of the community. It might be a diner, a bakery, a donut shop, or an espresso bar. Regardless, the community revolves in and around these cultural establishments. Coffee Roasters on K-Beach is one such establishment.

Quiet mornings in this coffee shop is where it all started. It would become an environment for maturing, developing, and growing for both my personal life and ministry career. From the first cup of coffee at 6:00

a.m. on my first day of the candidate trip and continued through four years of devotional writings, meetings, discipleship, mentorship, and numerous Gospel opportunities, God chose to use Coffee Roasters as my ministry training ground. And it's where I started to fall in love with Northern communities and the diverse people who live in them.

THE OWNER MAKES THE SHOP

As is typical in these cultural hubs, the owner, Micah, was a local himself. On the outside, he's a reserved, contemplative guy, who can appear somewhat stand-offish when you first meet him. But that's not really who Micah is. Upon deeper conversation with him, his heart for people, his passion for coffee, and his knowledge of Christ and the Church definitely shine through. Although he's local, Micah is well-traveled and has experienced a good portion of the outside world. During his younger years, he escaped small-town Alaska and met Shawna, who eventually became his wife.

Shawna is a caring, bubbly gal, who runs a small photography studio next to the shop. She was often seen making the rounds in the shop, remarking, "I just came in for a coffee, but then I run into so many people!" Micah would roll his eyes at this frequent comment, followed by a smirk. He realized that people are encouraged by her warm banter about the day's events. And let's be real; it balances out his more serious disposition. He would just go back to his work. In an almost choreographed dance, Shawna filled in every gap of Micah's rough exterior, and likewise, he seemed to provide stability into her care-free persona. Micah designed and maintained the mechanics of the shop, which was necessary. And although Shawna didn't work in the shop, she provided a vital role breathing life and energy into the place every time she walked through the door.

Micah's parents, Don and Jan, are pillars of the community, having invested many years into the Christian school down the road. They're a couple who put their faith first, having a remarkable ability to bring God into almost every conversation. Micah's siblings likewise invest in the community's well-being. Sister Cara is a massage therapist, and Brother Noah runs a counseling practice. They're a family who loves people, evidenced by how well-connected they are in the community. Moreover, Micah's family could be seen almost daily in the shop together as part of some informal family reunion. Such is the scene of a locally owned, small-town coffee shop; the owner's family becomes a permanent fixture—an almost irresistible feeling that becomes a part of the shop.

A few years after leaving Alaska, I dropped Micah a message to let him know I would be passing through. As I drove into the parking lot at Coffee Roasters, Micah had been watching for me. He was waiting outside my car door with my regular order—a sixteen-ounce drip (coffee) with room for cream. That is not happening at Starbucks or Tim Horton's. You can't artificially create or design places like Coffee Roasters and moments like that. These establishments happen because of the people in them, starting with the people who own them.

COFFEE SHOPS ARE COMMUNITY WELLS

For me, Coffee Roasters became the place where I would quench my thirst. They served excellent coffee, which I took in gallons of over my ministry to that community. But it was more than that. During those daily quiet mornings in that coffee shop, I also quenched my thirst for living water—the living water described in John's gospel by Jesus to the woman at the well: "You would have asked him, and he would have given you living water" (John 4:10).

Don't get me wrong, I had met Jesus many years before ever moving north and therefore, theologically had all the living water that I needed. But on those mornings, it seemed like there were only three people awake: me, the barista and Jesus. With the barista typically too busy to chit-chat, it made it easy for me to re-connect with Jesus, taking in another mug full of living water. In that shop at dawn, feeling Him quench my thirst, I read Scripture, prayed, thought and contemplated, and soon I began to write. That's where I would discover blogging, personal thoughts shared publicly. My passion and ability to write grew. Now, what started as a blog has become this book.

Quiet mornings don't last forever, though, do they? Soon enough, I began quenching my thirst for social interaction. As I've already mentioned, Coffee Roasters was always a hub for relationships—sometimes daily banter about politics, the weather, or retelling a hilarious story. Sometimes laughing so hard that Micah's gaze made you feel like you were about to get kicked out. But you never did.

On the flipside, other conversations delved deep into personal struggles and relational wounds. Ideally, topics that shouldn't be shared in such a public setting, but at a private table in the corner, where it seemed safe. It wasn't uncommon to see two or three people sharing in some heartache. Though you would never know the context of the conversation, you could see their pain. This coffee shop was a community interacting on the deepest level possible, through laughter and tears. All taking place at a variety of tables, day in and day out. As I watched and listened, I came to a new understanding of people, changing how I think and interact in any given community. Moreover, I came to a new understanding about how I do ministry.

The crux of this change is that coffee shops in Western culture are like the water wells of ancient days gone by. In the Old Testament, we read about the people of Israel going to the temple to meet with God. The community well, however, seemed to be the hub of relational interaction. Living under the New Covenant, many Christians want church buildings to be the hubs of life and relationship, but they're often not. Not for our communities, anyway. Sure, we do lots of church stuff in these buildings, but if we want to connect with the world around us, we have to admit that there is nothing in the church building that people physically need. Coffee, however, rightly or wrongly, has become the physical necessity for Western society. Due to this physical need, coffee shops have become the community hubs that churches are struggling to attain. There might be something there for us to ponder further.

MEETING FOR COFFEE

I was recently watching a remake of the popular series *Sherlock Holmes*. There's a brief scene in one of the episodes that made me smirk. A woman named Molly, who is evidently attracted to Holmes, asks, "I was wondering if you'd like to have coffee?" Still focused on the mystery at hand, Sherlock responds in his quirky manner, "Black, two sugars please." He clearly missed what was happening.[1]

Meeting for coffee has very little to do with coffee and everything to do with building a relationship. In our culture, it's the best mode of communication and should be embraced a lot more. I believe conflict would be avoided and dealt with more quickly if more coffee meetings were taking place. Our other modes of communication just aren't as effective.

Don't get me wrong. I love my smartphone, and I hold a great appreciation for all forms of technology and social media. When you live in the North, video calling is a necessary communication tool for connecting with friends, family, and colleagues who live *outside* (a Northern term for those living in Southern states and provinces.) Furthermore, after the 2020 pandemic, these video-based communication tools became mandatory. It took only a few months before people were craving physical, social interaction. People craved coffee meetings! There is something significant about meeting someone face to face. It makes a conversation so much more meaningful.

In John's second epistle, he's writing to a woman regarding church affairs. Then almost suddenly, John ends the letter with an important statement: "Though I have much to write to you, I would rather not use paper and ink.

---

1   *Sherlock*, season 1, episode 1, "A Study in Pink," directed by Paul McGuigan, written by Mark Gatiss, and Steven Moffat, featuring Benedict Cumberbatch, Martin Freeman, and Rupert Graves, aired July 25, 2010, BBC One.

Instead, I hope to come to you and talk face to face, so that our joy may be complete" (2 John 1:12).

Obviously, from the New Testament books, we see that written communication was vital and used frequently to maintain relationships and grow the Church. Nevertheless, think about how much more meaningful face-to-face communication would have been during John's day. Even short distances were long journeys for people who only had two choices—on foot or by pack animal. A personal visit and a shared meal with distant friends or colleagues would have been exciting—not to mention the incredible celebratory feeling if family were in town!

In this day and age, many church leaders are finding success by trying to fit their ministries into their cultural contexts. The concepts are often explained as being contemporary, relevant, or casual, yet the goal is the same. They're striving to reach the communities around them. They're striving to reach that community's culture. I believe this to be the right mindset and the biblical one. Just consider how much Jesus stepped into the culture around Him to reach people:

- When He called the first disciples, He spoke into their culture as a community of fishermen: "'Follow me, and I will make you fishers of men'" (Matt. 4:19).
- He used the community context of agriculture to highlight the need for evangelism: "'Therefore, pray earnestly to the Lord of the harvest to send out laborers into his harvest'" (Luke 10:2).
- And as we've already discussed, He used a community well to reach a woman outcast from culture: "'Everyone who drinks of this water will be thirsty again, but whoever drinks of the water that I will give him will never be thirsty again'" (John 4:13-14).

Before the 2020 pandemic, there was an increasing belief that to create a relevant culture was to create a digital culture. Looking back at blog posts from 2018 and 2019, it looked like we were headed in that direction. I definitely thought that physical and digital relationships were going to be interchangeable experiences. Then, we were all *forced* to became a digital culture. We quickly learned that even face-to-face video does not remotely equate to the face-to-face experience. We can't digitally replicate the authenticity behind the look, feel, sound, smell, and, of course, touch of another human.

Coming back to my original topic of discussion, I think there was one thing that we all craved during the pandemic. I would suggest that the pandemic solidified that one of the most culturally relevant requests in today's Western culture is to ask someone, "Want to meet up for coffee sometime?" That person will know that the coffee meeting will have very little to do with getting coffee and everything to do with an intentional, authentic, face-to-face interaction. It is a request for meaningful relationship.

GETTING OUT OF THE CHURCH OFFICE

I'm sure most would agree that pastors should spend a significant amount of time with people. A shepherd should spend at least some of his time with a few sheep. However, as a ministry grows, more people will start getting involved and showing up for church events and activities. With so many people in one place at one time, it can be very difficult for a pastor to get the facetime needed to develop authentic relationships. Ministry 101 suggests that by obtaining and training more ministry staff and volunteers, the pastor will spread his available impact. All the top-selling ministry books, courses, and resources would echo this principle.

I agree with this philosophy. I believe it's key to effective discipleship. I have tried my best to model this for the staff and volunteers with whom I've worked. I couldn't have pulled off a quarter of the ministry work that's been achieved over the years without them and this philosophy of ministry. But what about the people who never walk into the church building? Speaking now for smaller communities, and specifically Northern communities, there is a significant Gospel benefit to people knowing who the pastor is. More importantly, the pastor knowing who they are! Even with great ministry staff, it rarely helps the community at large to know who the pastor is. How can a pastor find balance?

Stepping back toward our analogy of the community well, where the people gather, I believe a pastor should try spending time in a coffee shop once in a while. By setting aside a day or two to work in this public setting, he becomes a visible fixture in the community. Eventually, he will become more authentic and approachable. By simply working alone in a coffee shop, he gives the general public some significant facetime needed to eventually bridge into a conversation. Believe it or not, people will approach you and start conversations with you. The familiarity of a face over weeks, then months, sends a message that "we belong here, so we should connect!" The pastor will provide that relational component to his community that rarely is achieved anywhere else in his ministry.

This may feel like an attack on the traditional view of pastoral roles, but I believe the days of community members randomly walking into a church office to "speak with a pastor" are over. And I would suggest this applies to any ministry worker. Meeting in local establishments can make all the difference in reaching a community for Jesus.

COFFEE CARD INVESTMENTS

When we start meeting at the well, investing in the spiritual growth of our community, it doesn't take long before people start noticing. Then they start investing in your investment. God's blessing soon pours out through unlikely, yet amazing, circumstances. One man in particular stands out in my mind. Let's call him Ken, as he'd prefer to stay anonymous.

Ken had decided early on to invest in my work at the community well. He witnessed the ministry that was unfolding at Coffee Roasters and felt led to bless that area of ministry. Every few weeks, Ken would carefully hold out his hand, revealing a couple of coffee cards. If there were people around, he'd pass them through a handshake or some other manner, careful not to let anyone see what he was doing. It always amazed me that just as I would start to run out of paying for coffee meetings with people, he was there to make sure I had the resources to continue this public ministry. It was such a blessing to me and the people with whom I interacted. Those coffee cards allowed me the opportunity to get out of the church office, providing a relaxed atmosphere for people to approach me outside the umbrella of religious institution. Through a simple act of giving, Ken greatly assisted in my time with church members and the community at large.

I would come to find out that Ken was an incredibly giving man, spiritually gifted with generosity. The proof came a couple of years later after Ken experienced some significant financial hardship. I remember sitting in the coffee shop with Ken and our lead pastor as he told us that he had lost his job. He was struggling to find work, only receiving odd jobs here and there but nothing with equivalent pay to his previous employment. I'm sure Keith assumed, like I did, that he wanted prayer for his situation. And he did, sort of. What he said next shocked us both. "I wanted to let you guys know that I believe God wants me to continue giving the same amount that I have been, even though I'm out of work. And I'd appreciate some prayer for that."

I assumed Ken wanted prayer for a new job, which of course we prayed for. That was the center of his request, though. He knew that he was about to face a financial challenge. He wanted prayer to sacrifice well, to remain giving to the church, missions, and coffee ministry at the same level he had been. And he did for months! Eventually, Ken found equal employment, receiving a permanent contract. Speaking about the ordeal now, he recounts the blessing of it all—the dependency he had on the Lord and the provisions that showed up right when he needed them.

Ken stands as an example to us all. First, he demonstrated how small acts of giving (like coffee cards) can invest in a greater Gospel work. Second, sometimes God calls us to sacrifice for the ministry to continue and, as Ken found out, to increase our trust in His provision.

THE DAY I BECAME A CELEBRITY

Remember that time that I returned for a visit to Coffee Roasters when Micah was waiting for me with my regular coffee order? That same day, something strange happened. After chit-chatting for quite some time with Micah while he worked, a barista whom I had never met came in to start her shift. She took over for Micah, and he and I sat in the corner to finish catching up. After he left, I decided to stay in the shop to get some writing done.

During this time, regulars started rolling in, picking up their coffee and noticing me. I knew so many of these folks! As is the case in small, Northern towns, people have their routines. Even though I had left a couple of years before, their routines continued. So, there I was again, to catch up with each person where I left off. Almost every one of them stopped for at least ten minutes to chat and catch up. It was an amazing morning!

Here's where it got weird, though. After the morning rush was over and everyone had gone to work, Coffee Roasters was experiencing the mid-morning lull before the 10:00 a.m. coffee break hit. It was quiet, and I was typing away.

Then I heard a soft voice from behind the counter. "Excuse me?" It was the barista—the gal I had never met. (And Micah, being Micah, never introduced me.)

"Hi!" I looked up from my laptop, expecting her to ask if I'd like more coffee or perhaps a baked good that, from the smell, had just come out of the oven.

"Are you a celebrity?" she asked.

"Excuse me?" I was sure I didn't hear her correctly.

"Are you a celebrity or something like that?" she asked again, trying to clarify her question.

"No. Why?" I was a little surprised that I had heard her correctly the first time.

"Well, everyone who walks in here knows who you are, but I've never seen you before!"

"Oh! No, I used to be a pastor here. Well, not here in Coffee Roasters, but here on the Peninsula. And I spent a lot of time in this shop, meeting with people. My name's Jeremy. What's yours?"

She gave me her name and a somewhat obligated, "Nice to meet you."

Then she was immediately interested in getting back to work, clearly unimpressed since she had expected to meet a celebrity but was disappointed to have just met a pastor.

This odd interaction made me laugh, as I pondered it for a while. Thinking about the past two hours from the barista's perspective, it made sense. Almost every single person who walked in that morning recognized me and at least said hello if they were in a hurry. And most of them lit up with a smile and immediately walked over to me. All the while, the barista was having serious FOMO (fear of missing out). *Who is that guy?* she must have thought to herself over and over again. I was shocked that she never asked any of the customers or texted Micah. Maybe she thought she should have known.

This strange situation proves my point, though, doesn't it? I had become a permanent fixture, a part of the community well. Even after I had been gone for a few years, I was able to jump right back in, connecting with so many people with whom I had shared numerous relational moments. It was a huge blessing to see everyone, but the interaction with the barista was the greater blessing. It was a confirmation that if you put the time in, you can belong.

FINDING YOUR COMMUNITY WELL

Where is your community watering hole? In your town, where do the people congregate naturally? If I were coming into your neighborhood, where would you suggest we meet for coffee? It's time to establish that location. It's time to start investing some time in your community well.

If you only have a desktop computer, it's time to invest in a laptop or at least a tablet. Make your work mobile so that people see you more frequently. Help them wonder who you are and what you do. Be around so much that they feel an internal obligation to get to know you. Then it'll happen. You will belong there. And once you belong there, people will expect to see you there. They'll start small talk, chat about the weather, or bring up current community events. It's at this point that you can make or break the ministry potential of having a place at the well. Though difficult at first, close your laptop and ask them to sit down. Regardless of the sermon, lesson plan, or project you're working on, turn the tablet over. Ask them to sit down.

God will have brought you that person, at that time, in that place. Embrace the interruption! Embrace the chance to meet someone new or reconnect with someone you already know. Accept the fact that it's highly unlikely that this person was going to walk into the church office and ask to speak with you. Remind yourself of that fact. This interruption is why you made the switch to the well in the first place. The time is now; find your community well.

SMALL TOWN COFFEE ROASTERS

As I was finalizing this chapter, Micah published a short video message on social media explaining that Coffee Roasters had been sold. It shocked me, and I felt a bit sad. As I mentioned previously, the feel of local establishments is somewhat connected to the owner. With new ownership, the feel might change, but I'm sure Small Town Coffee Roasters will remain the K-Beach community well. The same people, and perhaps new people, will find its refreshment, both physically through great coffee and relationally through great conversation. Lord willing, the Gospel will still be weaved in and out of those tables as believers share the truth of Jesus while enjoying another sixteen-ounce drip of great coffee.

CHAPTER FIVE

MINISTRY IS A TEAM SPORT: COACHES AND CAPTAINS

"Two are better than one, because they have a good reward for their toil.
For if they fall, one will lift up his fellow. But woe to him who is alone
when he falls and has not another to lift him up!"

Ecclesiastes 4:9-10

"You'll do it because I'm your boss." Believe it or not, this used to be a motivating statement in previous generations. Okay, maybe *motivating* isn't the right word, but it worked. It produced action through much of the Western world for many decades. Then everything shifted. The shift started with Gen-X but ramped up through the millennial generation. Now that millennials are entrenched in the working world, this kind of statement is a sure-fire way to get any team member to quit. Note that I said *team member*, not *employee*. And this concept should be issued ten-fold for those of us who are directing any type of ministry. This concept should be issued a hundred-fold for those of us who are directing ministry in small communities. If we desire to motivate our teams, we'll need to be coaches, not bosses.

HOW TO COACH AND NOT BOSS

When we look at the Gospels, we can see Jesus embracing a coach-like ministry with His disciples. He didn't simply sit in the synagogue all day, sending the disciples out to perform duties. That would be a very boss-like role. Instead, Jesus brought them along, showing them how to live out ministry, coaching them along the way. There were times of joy, sadness, and even rebuke. These were all shared within the team of disciples. In all aspects of ministry, Jesus was the perfect example of what a coach should be for his team.

Excluding professional sports, most coaches are tasked with motivating a team of people, who are working hard for minimal pay or no payment whatsoever. For the small-town coach, even finding finances for equipment is a challenge. Many who serve in ministry work on a humble salary or serve as a volunteer. Small-town church budgets are often slim, with limited resources to invest in each ministry area. Coaches and ministry leaders are, therefore, compelled to motivate their teams to and for something greater. The mission is the motivator, not the money. I believe ministry leaders who think and act like coaches will experience greater success. Once again, this concept is amplified in a small community context.

What does a ministry coach look like? They generally acknowledge extra effort. Even when the slightest display of hard work or increased drive is given, a coach is excellent at recognizing it. This is an ongoing, consistent practice—kind of like hearing an "attaboy" from the senior pastor.

First, ministry coaches celebrate wins. When a milestone has been hit, a coach doesn't bask in self-gratification. It's not about the great coach he or she is; it's about how hard the team worked to achieve that win. Therefore, the jubilant celebration should be given over to the team and, ultimately, given to Christ because the team has advanced the mission.

Second, ministry coaches rise out of defeat. This is where coaching gets to shine. When morale is low and everything seems against the team, a coach doesn't cocoon himself in his office. He gathers the team, looks them straight in the eye, takes ownership of the defeat, then rallies them back to the mission. A great coach will take all the value and self-worth that has been lost through defeat and bring it back to the team with vigor. The team is once again empowered and ready to strive forward.

A ministry coach is nothing without the ministry team. It's an interdependent relationship. We can't ever forget that. And with localized churches within small communities, where everyone seems to know everyone else, the interdependent relationships are a fact of life. Coaches can't afford to be bosses in these settings. Ministry, and the mission, will be lost.

BECOMING A CAPTAIN

Soon after arriving in Alaska, I needed to figure out how to build and motivate a ministry team. Keep in mind, this was my first official pastoral position. The senior pastor and our elders had an influence on my role, coaching me as I began to lead and facilitate ministry. Something was still missing, though. Who could specifically coach my decisions within my area of student ministry? Who had the experience to coach me as a youth pastor?

When starting into a new leadership position, it's important to ask about that ministry's history. Once again, I would amplify this concept within the small community context. Small-town ministries always have a few skeletons in the closet, but they usually have a few heroes as well. At some point, newcomers will be sized up in a comparison against these past leaders. I might as well get to know a bit about them! So, I started trying to find out who the key players were from the past. What were the big wins and big losses? What kind of people excelled in that role, and who had a significant influence?

Many of these conversations took place within the first couple of months. With each account I listened to, there was one person who continued to have rave reviews on their success within the role that I was taking on. No matter who I spoke with, one name kept rising to the surface as a leader of the youth ministry golden years: Carmen. The surprising part for me was that Carmen was a woman. Not that I don't think women can be effective in ministry leadership. I was just surprised because many churches in smaller communities shy away from hiring female leaders, especially within a fairly conservative church like ours in a predominantly conservative culture like Alaska. Therefore, I assumed she must have been an extremely talented leader!

Soon enough, the senior pastor found all of Carmen's old files and passed them on to me. As I scanned through various documents, I saw that she was steadfast in her work. Clearly, from the content I was reading, she had seen a huge amount of success during her term. Unfortunately, as is the case with most successful leaders, she had moved on to new places with new opportunities. Carmen no longer attended the church, nor lived in the area, but God is faithful!

It wasn't long before there were rumors that Carmen would be returning to the area. Furthermore, she planned to attend our church and work somewhere in the community. I'll be honest, this news was a bit threatening for me at first. I knew it would be difficult for people not to compare what Carmen had accomplished with the ministry plans that I was about to set into motion. Connecting with her became my top priority.

Once Carmen arrived, we headed down to Coffee Roasters for a meet-and-greet. We had a great time discussing the ministry's past, present, and future. I realized almost immediately that she needed to become one of my coaches. She would help our ministry succeed. Carmen knew the culture of our state, our community, and our church. I knew that by running game plans by her before implementing them, it would save me a lot of lost games and increase our wins.

Sometimes, ministry leaders have to move from the position of the coach into the position of captain. Carmen's willingness to become a ministry coach helped me become a great captain. She was willing to encourage, challenge, and if needed, rebuke me. She was an amazing asset to my ministry. I took great weight in her suggestions and ideas. I was constantly aware that she had more successful years of student ministry at that church and in that community than anyone else I had connections with.

Maybe you have a great ministry team that you're coaching well. That's fantastic! That should be celebrated, but don't forget that you're not only on the sidelines; you're also in the game. There is always a limited supply of people and resources. We leaders are called to coach the team, but we're also putting forth just as much physical, emotional, mental, and spiritual effort. Depending on your area of ministry and leadership, you may find yourself in a situation where you need to move from coaching to the position of captain. There may come a time when you have to step out on the field and put yourself under the counsel of a coach.

Even Jesus, Who needed no coaching, chose to place Himself under the guidance of the Father. He said, "For I have come down from heaven, not to do my own will but the will of him who sent me" (John 6:38). Jesus came to earth, joined the field of men, becoming the great Captain (the example), calling all people to follow Him. Then in the early mornings and late nights, Jesus spent time alone in prayer, seeking the counsel and comfort of the One Who sent Him (Matt. 14:23; Mark 1:35; Luke 5:16).

We, too, should seek our heavenly Father's guidance and coaching before we ever seek the guidance of anyone else. Once counsel is received from the Father, we can still seek help with the work of the ministry. This isn't a bad thing, as long as we carefully select the right people to coach us along the way.

FINDING AN ASSISTANT CAPTAIN

Growth happens, often before you're ready for it. Soon enough, a ministry leader can be consumed by the day-to-day details that have nothing to do with the overall vision work that should be taking place. These details can start to affect the team as well. Team members may start questioning the coach or captain, realizing that they've lost focus, juggling the increasing number of roles and responsibilities. Team members may even start to drop off the roster to become free agents for other teams and ministry areas. As leaders, we should be sensitive to this shift, if and when it happens. It's at this point that we need to start looking for an assistant captain.

It was a chilly Sunday morning in February. As Pastor Keith wrapped up his sermon, he explained that we would be having a couple of scheduled baptisms to conclude our service. Then he gave an open invitation to anyone else who would like to be baptized, stating that they could come forward during the next song. Almost immediately, a young woman named Morgan stepped forward without hesitation. Though she was new to our church and didn't have a swimsuit or extra clothes to change into, she was going to be baptized. There was more to know about this young girl who so easily faded into our congregation, yet rose with conviction on that day. I was persuaded that I had to get to know her.

Within weeks, Morgan and I connected. It turned out that she had recently moved to small-town Alaska from Washington State to start her adult life. I was excited to hear that she had a passion for Jesus and a desire to serve Him as soon as possible. And serve she did! Her energy level and excitement were addicting. My creativity flourished as she spent more time around our church, helping me prepare and facilitate a variety of events. She was young and had lots to learn about working with people, but she was faithful. She poured her time into ministry, striving to move forward in her relational skills and biblical knowledge. Needless to say, she impressed me time and time again.

I have to say it again: God is faithful! I soon realized that He had provided us with an amazing assistant captain. Morgan had already put more than enough time in to prove her worth. Not only was she engaged with our student ministry, but it also seemed like every spare moment was spent serving our church and the community as a whole. She exuded passion for her ministry work and for life in general. Conversations with her energized me to become a better leader.

As you can imagine, as a young leader, she was a work in progress. But I was, too. People who are a work in progress, that are willing to progress, typically have loads of passion. They're typically worth investing in, providing a great environment for fresh ministry ideas. These are the people who make excellent assistant captains.

It didn't take long before the obvious next step was to hire her. Morgan's role gradually moved from ten hours per week to twenty hours. If it weren't for budget constraints, we could have easily hired her full-time, and she would have fulfilled several roles and responsibilities in and through our church. She took on many of the tasks that were important but were pulling me away from major projects and vision-casting.

Going back to the example that Jesus set for us, we can see Scripture seems to indicate that Peter, James, and John were an inner circle of disciples (Matt. 26:37; Mark 9:2). Keeping with our team metaphor, these were Jesus' assistant captains. Look at Peter's life specifically. He was the perfect example of a work in progress.

- Peter had the passion to jump out of a boat and walk on water, just to be overcome with fear and lose faith (Matt. 14:30).
- Peter had the zeal to rebuke Jesus after He foretold His execution and then was embarrassed as Jesus put him in his place (Matt 16:21-23).
- After Jesus predicts Peter's denial, he responds resolute that he will stand firm (Matt. 26:33-35) just to face the shame and sorrow of his weakness (Luke 22:54-62).

Surely from this evidence, Peter would not be worth the investment, where, in fact, the opposite is true. Because of this evidence, Peter's worth the investment. So much so, that Jesus not only reinstates Peter after his massive moral failure (John 21:15-19), He moves him up the roster to the position of captain. Jesus ends up passing His ministry on to Peter, who became a launching point for the Church after the Ascension. "And I tell you, you are Peter, and on this rock I will build my church, and the gates of hell shall not prevail against it. I will give you the keys of the kingdom of heaven, and whatever you bind on earth shall be bound in heaven, and whatever you loose on earth shall be loosed in heaven" (Matt. 16:18-19).

GAINING A TEAM PERSPECTIVE

God used Carmen and Morgan to give me a team mindset for ministry. Since then, and throughout my work, He has continued to bring me coaches, captains, and assistant captains. I've grown to love, appreciate, and cherish every one of them. Each individual answered God's call to lead ministry, embracing their gifts and abilities, choosing to use them for His Kingdom purposes. Now, as a lead pastor, I have many more opportunities to coach. I receive blessing after blessing, witnessing the leadership process unfold, as each leader takes their place as captain or assistant captain over their own ministry teams. Some of them have been paid staff, even as low as five to ten hours a week. Others remain as volunteer leaders. And yet all of them understand and embrace a team perspective within their ministries. It is so much fun to journey with these emerging leaders!

This is one of the unique pieces to the small-town church. Instead of the senior and associate pastor being the staff team, it's a mixed bag of potential. If you're not embracing it, you're missing out. Within the ministry, we should make every effort to implement team perspectives. To be sure, being on a team is hard work. There are occasional losses. And I know that I've had my fair share. I've failed my team more times than I want to admit.

Thankfully, the teams that I've been a part of have always had grace for me as a leader. I have experienced what the preacher in Ecclesiastes describes: "Two are better than one, because they have a good reward for their toil. For if they fall, one will lift up his fellow" (Eccl. 4:9-10a). I've seen it lived out and experienced it. Along with my coaches and assistant captains by my side, we and the team rolled through and learned together.

Maybe you're in this position. Maybe you've been trying to sustain your ministry without outside help or accountability. Perhaps you started with a great team, but you've slipped into a boss-like state. Maybe your team members are moving on to other ministries. Or worse, they're moving on to other churches.

Regardless of the challenges you face, bring in quality people to share the load. And quality doesn't mean people who always agree with you. Depending on your situation, it may be time to find and submit to a coach. It may be time to rethink some of your boss-like behaviors. It may be time to obtain some key players. It may be time to accept some of your faults and ask forgiveness. It'll be tough, but it might just bring back some key players. It's time for renewal, and it's time for growth. It's time to gain a team perspective.

CHAPTER SIX

PINK PIXIES WORK THE BEST

"O Lord, how manifold are your works! In wisdom have you made them all;
the earth is full of your creatures."

Psalms 104:24

When's the last time you went outside to play? Children love being outside. Regardless of the season, when mom or dad offers up the opportunity to go play outside, almost every little boy and girl jump at the chance. Watching kids outside is so much fun. They chirp back at the birds in the trees, dig in the garden to add some new creepy-crawly to their collection, or just lie in the grass finding shapes in the clouds. Rain or snow won't stop kids from wanting to be outside either. If anything, it improves the experience! Puddles or snow piles provide even more wonder to the overall backyard experience.

Then one day, the boundaries of the backyard are broken. The child reaches the stage where the circle of adventure is widened past the backyard and into the local park or playground. There are now loads of new friends with whom to play games and enjoy the incredible land of outside.

Then the boundaries widen again when a child takes their first trip to a national park, nature reserve, or other protected recreation area—untouched wilderness with more fascination than any child could take in at one time. New trees, new plants, new bugs, and even new animals from time to time. And these animals don't wear collars! It's at this point where Mom or Dad may look at each other and say, "If only we could look at the world through their eyes! Wouldn't that be great?"

Unfortunately, something strange happens to most of us near adulthood. Somehow, the enjoyment of playing outside loses its luster. All of a sudden, going outside starts to depend on the weather or temperature or even the ratio of sunlight to clouds. It becomes something we have to do for physical health reasons instead of enjoyment. We try to tell ourselves, "I really should go out and get some exercise. The fresh air would do me good." Regardless of our abundant access to transportation and numerous natural wonders, our childhood thrills of playing outside have suddenly become a chore. Even though most of us greatly appreciate and are in awe of the majestic world that God has created, we tend to look at it through the lens of social media.

CONNECTING WITH CREATION

According to Paul's letter to the Romans, creation should point anyone and everyone in God's direction. "For his invisible attributes, namely, his eternal power and divine nature, have been clearly perceived, ever since the creation of the world, in the things that have been made. So they are without excuse" (Rom. 1:20).

What if refusing to play outside had greater risks than just our physical health? What if there were serious spiritual implications to not connecting with the created world? What if we're not getting the full dose of "his invisible attributes" and "divine nature" by simply spending two weeks a year on a beach somewhere?

The concept of taking time to check out of work life and enjoy God's creation has always been my desire. Sadly, I am amazed at how quickly busy schedules, sermon prep, and project deadlines will keep me indoors. When I do get outside, however, there is something life-giving about creation experiences. They bring me back to the magnitude and might of our heavenly Father. They allow me to reflect on current trials within a setting that proves

God's hand will sustain me. For those of you who struggle with pride, as I do, the created world can bring us back down from our high places. We are humbled by our Creator's innovation and artistic design. We are reminded just how small we are.

In larger communities, city planners are doing their best to create natural spaces within the urban environment. These types of spaces are an integral part of a city's well-being. Though for city folk who desire some untouched creation, there's usually quite a bit of planning involved and some distance to be traveled to experience it. On the flipside, living in a smaller community usually carries the benefit of natural beauty close by. For those of us who are blessed to live in these types of communities are often a short drive or walk away. It may be a forest, a mountain, or a meadow, a lake, a river, or maybe even a small, meandering stream running through the valley where the town is located. Each of these created ecosystems holds a wealth of God's invisible attributes, revealing His power and nature every single day.

Regardless of where we're located, finding some untouched creation and spending time there can greatly impact our walk with Jesus. For the pastor or ministry leader, I believe something significant can be obtained from entering into creation on a more regular basis. If we isolate ourselves from the created world, we're neglecting some valuable leadership benefits that God has planned for us. I would suggest that time in creation will increase our overall ministry potential. We'll remember that in Jesus, "All things were made through him, and without him was not any thing made that was made" (John 1:3). In awe, we will be humbled into servanthood to the One Who spoke these magnificent places into existence.

Specific to my experience, the North holds an abundance of created wonders. Overall, serving in Northern communities has provided plenty of opportunities to witness God's spectacular, yet truly wild, nature within His creation. Through a few keys experiences, I have gained firsthand insight into His handiwork and character.

MARINE LIFE AND GOD'S FAITHFULNESS

Marine environments are created ecosystems that have always fascinated me. Even a small pond has proven to be a place of wonder. Growing up in Southern Ontario, Canada, I was provided with numerous experiences in a variety of watersheds and tributaries. My dad taught my brothers and me how to fish at an early age. In the summer, I remember riding our bikes to the outskirts of town. From there, we'd either follow a trail through the bush or head down the train tracks to a bridge over a creek. We'd have a fire, catch frogs, and fish. We loved that spot and spent hours there. It was at that creek where I caught my first fish—without my dad present, that is. It was a good-sized fish, and I was so excited! And it taught me a valuable lesson about follow-through.

If you've never been shore fishing before, once the fish has been reeled in and the hook is removed, the fish is placed on line or chain called a "stringer." A stringer can typically hold a few or a dozen fish depending on the size. Now, when one places a fish on a stringer, this is just the first step. Tying the other end of the stringer to a tree or rock is a fairly critical step to keeping said fish. As I watched my fish swim away with a long nylon cord hanging from its gill, I suddenly realized I had made a terrible error. Before I could react and jump in, the fish (and my stringer) were gone. I felt devastated on multiple levels!

First, I lost the fish. Second, that fish wasn't going to survive attached to a stringer. Third, I lost the stringer my dad had given me. Fourth, in hindsight, I polluted my favorite creek with a nylon cord.

I have never placed a fish on a stringer again without reliving that moment in my mind's eye. "Jeremy, don't get so excited that you forget about follow-through!"

Moving to Alaska gave me my first opportunity to live close to the ocean. I had visited coastal places before, but living near the sea provided an abundance of joy and wonder. My appreciation for marine life increased ten-fold as our family had opportunities to view whales, porpoises, seals, otters, and a variety of fish and sea creatures. Many of the latter ended up on our table for dinner. We enjoyed digging clams on the beach and pulling mussels off the rocks during low tide. Soon, these shelled gems would be fried or boiled and plunged into melted butter. Salmon, which was a delicacy back home, was common and abundant table fare. In my opinion, it is best served baked in lemon juice and fresh dill.

Alaska's Kenai Peninsula holds some of the largest salmon runs in the world, seeing hundreds of thousands of fish each year, returning to spawn. Learning to fish during these massive runs was a thrill! Depending on the run, I might be "flippin' for Reds" (short-casting a fly for Sockeye), "runnin' Spin-n-Glows for Kings" (trolling or anchored with a baited spinning rig), or "soakin' eggs for Silvers" (drifting with cured eggs in an egg-loop-hook). And when all else fails, there's always "throwin' Pixies" (casting a salmon-specific lure called a "Pixie"). By the way, pink pixies work the best!

Now that you know some Kenai Peninsula salmon fishing lingo, I want to come back to the spawn itself. Through a miraculous process of instinct that can only truly be explained through the majesty of God's handiwork, salmon return each year to the same place. That's right; after a few years in the open ocean, growing in size and strength, they return to the very same place where their lives began. This is without any cognitive ability to remember such a place. Never mind remembering the actual journey to find their way back.

Salmon are a created wonder that leave evolutionary theorists scratching their heads. There are many theories, but science has yet to come up with a definitive reason why salmon return to the exact same spot. Creation, however, gives us a better answer. The more I've watched and fished each of the West Coast salmon species, the more they have become a tangible weapon to battle my days of doubt. Our Creator is truly good and faithful, naturally bringing this delicious and nutritious food source back to the very place it started.

Moreover, it's a perfect circle of life that God would hardwire salmon to return because an entire ecosystem branches out from their return. During and after the salmon spawn, these fish feed almost every living thing along the river systems, top to bottom, from the largest grizzly bear to the smallest micro-organism. Salmon prove to me God's goodness and faithfulness in designing miraculous natural systems, not just to display His glory but also for our benefit and pleasure—a beautiful example of God's common grace poured out for us each and every year.

"FISH ON!"

The biggest of Pacific salmon is called the King, technically known as the Chinook salmon. The Kenai Peninsula is famous for containing some of the largest King salmon stock in the world. Although I had battled my share of Northern Pike back in Ontario, none of them adequately prepared me for the fight of a Kenai Peninsula King, a distinct characteristic being its strike. Unlike many other fish species that tend to bump a lure or nose the bait before taking it, the King wastes no time in snatching what it wants. The strike is typically fast and furious, the rod tip driving toward the surface of the water in an instant. And once that rod tip has crashed, the first to notice cries out, "Fish on!"

In an instant, a boat full of dazed fishermen become an all-hands-on-deck naval crew. An immediate expectation is that all other lines are reeled in as fast as humanly possible and rods stowed. This prevents a *tie-up* and, inevitably, a fish lost. The man on the prop (short for a propeller, or motor) stands at attention. He keeps one eye on the scene in the boat and the other eye downriver on what lies ahead. He navigates in such a way as to avoid any river feature that may hinder the catch. Third position yells, "I got net!" Even though the fight has just started, he's ready for the moment the fish is brought within arm's reach of the boat.

Any other fisherman should be laser-focused on the constant movement of themselves and gear, keeping the path clear for the man tied into the King. That fish will swing the line to and fro, under the boat, and over the heads of the fishermen. One learns an instinctive way to switch boat positions without hindrance, nor without being told. Lastly, and perhaps most importantly, someone had better have a phone, either already recording the fight or ready to snap the first glance of the beast.

Spending time in a fishing boat is a blessing. The fresh air, recreation, and time spent with friends or family hold incredible value. There are also some important lessons to be learned, especially from those battles with the big fish. For me, taking on a King salmon helped me understand how a ministry should function. It's not a pleasure cruise where staff catch the fish, cook it, and serve it up for your pleasure and enjoyment. It's an all-hands-on-deck experience! Every person has a specific role or responsibility that must take place to take on that challenge and obtain the prize. It may be a crisis that has happened in the community or a strategic ministry project that can only take place with full participation. Once the rallying cry goes out, it's "Fish on!" and time to jump into action.

WILD GAME AND GOD'S PROVISION

Before moving north, I had always fished but never hunted. Upon my arrival to Alaska, I was able to carry a firearm right away without any paperwork. A few visits to the gravel pit for target shooting and I was ready to start filling the freezer! I stuck to small game hunting in the beginning: spruce hens (grouse) and snowshoe hare (rabbit).

My oldest son, Jude, and I would venture out into the woods behind our house and seek out the elusive snowshoe. They'll sit motionless under a spruce tree, completely camouflaged, except for the deep, dark eye that's often the only give-away. Sometimes, they'll dart out right beside you because you've wandered right on top of them without ever noticing. I remember when Jude brought home his first rabbit puffed up with pride and excited to show Nicole his prize. He had moved from a member of the family to a provider for the family. Since then, our boys have brought home quite a few rabbits and grouse.

On my first big game hunt, I was invited out to harvest a black bear with my friend Pat from our church. At that time, I couldn't pull the trigger, due to not having my big game tags. The experience was epic, anyway. It was early spring, and the bear was just waking from hibernation. The goal was to hike up to a mountain lake and fish for grayling, while glassing (using a scope or binoculars) on the mountainsides where the sun had started to bring out vegetation. Bears often graze on south-facing slopes to get their digestion moving after the long winter's nap. Plants are also a lot easier to chase down when the fat and muscle reserves are low. We were hoping to spot a bear worth shooting. Sure enough, we did!

We hadn't been fishing for more than ten minutes when Pat pointed it out. We watched a black spot meander across the mountainside. The hunt was on. I hung back while Pat slowly tracked forward to get a clear shot. A couple of loud cracks later, the black spot tumbled down into a patch of Alder bushes. After a long slug of bush-whacking up to the kill site, we were standing over the biggest black bear that he or I had ever seen.

The bear was six feet in length from nose to tail and easily weighed three hundred pounds. (For any hunters or marksman out there, Pat used a seven-millimeter Remington Magnum, shooting a 140-grain bullet.) We ended up packing out the head, the rug, and eighty-five pounds of meat. Since Pat was only interested in the fur, he gave me the meat for helping him with the hunt. Packing out an extra eighty-five pounds was a challenge, but the experience as a whole was worth every minute of struggle. Within a few days, our family had bear roasts and pepperettes in the freezer.

Since then, God has given me the blessing of harvesting my own black bear and small grizzly. He has also provided a moose, and I'm looking forward to harvesting a bison this spring. Our family will continue to harvest animals, providing an ample supply of wild game on our dinner table. In general, I think small communities have a better handle on food provision when compared to larger communities where food is predominately purchased from a grocery store. The wide-open spaces often connected to smaller communities provide an opportunity to harvest from the wild or farm. People living in small towns and villages often know a thing or two about farming the land, raising livestock, or hunting sections of local wilderness.

There's a strong connection between our plight for food and God's provision of that food. Communities of every size have conversations about the weather and economy. And yet the link between these two topics seems to become greater as the community gets smaller. The amount of precipitation can make or break the season's crop. Temperature swings can change the migration of wildlife in a particular hunting zone. The price of grain or livestock can have a serious impact on local shared wealth. There may be a prayer or two offered up during any and all of these scenarios.

Please don't misunderstand what I'm saying. I am not saying that larger communities don't have a dependency on God's provision. I'm not saying that people living in big cities blindly make purchases without any concept of the greater economic system. I'm not saying that they don't understand where their resources come from. I do believe they feel the pressure of loss and the blessing of gain within food-based products and services. On some level, I believe they get it, but perhaps not completely.

Having lived in both circumstances, there is something unique that takes place as a family gathers around the dinner table in the dead of winter over a moose roast that God blessed them with during the fall hunt. The prayer of thanksgiving that takes place over that table feels different. Somehow, it carries a weightier reverence for the Creator and Sustainer of all life. God's provision of that wild game is appreciated in the greatest of capacities. I'm telling you, something changes.

RETREATING INTO CREATION

Have you spent one too many days entrenched in industry and technology? Perhaps you've forgotten the last time you saw something natural, other than the dandelions in your front yard or the cactus that sits on the corner of your desk. Maybe your relationships both with God and with the people around you are starting to feel as mechanical as the everyday comforts that you can't seem to live without. If this is your life, it's time to retreat!

Regardless of the church, ministry, or community you live in and serve, there is great value in connecting with creation. It may be based on personally connecting with Jesus through a day trip, or it may be an extended solo journey into His untouched handiwork. It might be a group outing with friends or family to enjoy the Creator's handiwork together. I promise you that building relationships and making memories within the wonder of His natural world is worth the effort!

Your retreat might be found in a planned visit to a farm or ranch. Not just as a spectator but to assist in the harvest or care for livestock. You will gain a better appreciation for the blessings that God lavishes upon us. Maybe your retreat brings with it a huge step outside your comfort zone to embrace a fishing or hunting excursion. Why not experience what it's like to harvest a fish or animal right from the Creator's hand? Then feel the weighty blessing of provision as you give thanks over it and enjoy its flavor and sustenance with friends and family around the dinner table.

Whichever purposeful retreat you decide on, it will be incredibly beneficial both to your personal walk within this world and your spiritual journey with Jesus. Your daily tasks and responsibilities will seem trivial. Your awareness of God's sovereignty will be heightened. Your humility before God's power and might will silence internal pride. Your appreciation for your very breath will bring about thanksgiving. Plan a purposeful retreat into creation today.

PART THREE

GOD'S WORK IN THE NORTH

CHAPTER SEVEN

IT WAS AN EPIC WIN

"So, being affectionately desirous of you, we were ready to share with you
not only the gospel of God but also our own selves,
because you had become very dear to us."

1 Thessalonians 2:8

The Good News of Jesus Christ should be at the forefront of our ministry efforts. Although it may look very different, depending on the size of the community, we all have to answer the same questions that the apostle Paul posed to the Church two thousand years ago: "How then will they call on him in whom they have not believed? And how are they to believe in him of whom they have never heard? And how are they to hear without someone preaching" (Rom. 10:14). Every local church is called to reach their own community with the Gospel, and they have to figure out how they're going to make that happen.

In years past, conferences and concerts were great opportunities to present the Gospel to large groups of people. Historically, they may have been referred to as "revivals." Growing up in southern Ontario, I had unique opportunities within a few hours' drive in Toronto, Detroit, and Buffalo. They drew people from within those cities but also from the surrounding communities. Living in a smaller city, Sarnia, we would load into a van or bus, and the road trip would become part of the experience. Sometimes, the fact that we were headed to the big city made the initiation more appealing for skeptics who might not have accepted an invitation to a church service.

This works, of course, if there's a large urban center within a few hours' drive. How far is too far? I remember the excitement when an event was being held in Detroit instead of Toronto because it shaved an hour off the trip. Moving north taught me that an hour's drive is relative to what is considered normal. Moreover, people who live in the North prove the old adage, "Where there's a will, there's a way!"

FUSION ALASKA

One of the greatest events in the North is a youth conference in Anchorage called Fusion Alaska. While serving in Alaska, I had the pleasure of bringing students to this event and even leading a few break-out sessions. Coming up from the Kenai Peninsula was not a huge journey. However, I was shocked to see how far church leaders would be willing to drive to bring students from their distant community to this event. What began as a youth conference for the big city of Anchorage and surrounding area spread to become a state-wide youth conference. Eventually, Fusion drew Canadians from the Yukon, becoming an internationally attended event. In case you're unfamiliar with the area, it's over seven hundred miles and over twelve hours of driving from Whitehorse, Yukon, to Anchorage, Alaska.

Maybe you're wondering, "Why would someone drive twelve hours to attend an event?" Part of it is like I said—Northerners are known to live out the adage, "Where there's a will, there's a way!" However, the deeper answer is as old as the Church. For over a decade of hosting, Fusion has remained Gospel-centered in everything they do. That means that not only do they book Gospel-motivated speakers and artists, but also that the staff and volunteers are laser-focused on bringing the Good News of Jesus to every student who attends. Many of these students travel from communities of which most people around the world have never even heard. And every year, at least a dozen students meet Jesus for the first time at Fusion.

I would add one last reason, and perhaps a reminder to us all, that Gospel-centered leaders create Gospel-centered organizations. Having served under both directors of Fusion Alaska, Darryl Nelson and Wesley Arnes, I can say that without a doubt, both of these men live out the Gospel—not only in what they do, but also in who they are. This, of course, will lead to God's blessing but also shows that these men have found favor with Christian leaders throughout the North and beyond. Their Gospel focus has created trust in who they are, who they lead, and which events they host and facilitate. Church leaders have more than enough evidence to justify the cost of time, resources, and distance to travel.

KENAI COLLABORATION

Once I landed in the North, I found a great way to stay connected. The Kenai Peninsula Youth Network (KPYN) was an amazing resource for connection and collaboration. The group was focused on reaching students for Christ, as well as supporting each other in prayer and encouragement. The interesting component was that the members of the network weren't all pastors and ministers. As I stated in an earlier chapter, many small community churches don't have the funds to hire a full-time, or even a part-time, pastor. So, hiring youth ministry staff is a definite luxury. As we assembled, we were a group of staff and volunteer leaders, all of us directing our individual student ministries, yet collaborating as a whole. It was incredible the network of resources brought together for the greater Gospel mission.

Many of the smaller churches in the Network had collaborated in the past to attend Fusion, renting vans and buses together, or booking group rates for hotel rooms. Then one day, a few of us began to ask, "Big events can be held in the big city, but what would it take for us to host something big here on the Peninsula?" This question would lead our small network of youth leaders down a road that would become an epic win for our local churches and the community.

The *why* was clear, driven out of why we were connecting regularly in the first place. We wanted to bring the hope of Jesus to students on the Kenai Peninsula. The *what* became clear in the early stages of planning. It would be a concert-style event, but we'd need a name that could really capture a student's attention.

For decades, pop culture has created buzz words and catch phrases that teenagers cling to and typically overuse. Our parents may have used the term "groovy threads" to complement each other's clothing. I definitely remember using the term "sweet kicks" every time I saw someone wearing a pair of expensive sneakers. For youth leaders at the time, we knew that everything a teenager approved of was considered "epic." And if they enjoyed something, it was a "win." Therefore, if we were going to set the bar high, only one pop culture catch phrase would suffice.

EPIC WIN

Epic Win would be a dual-stage concert event. The main stage environment would have spotlights and big sound, featuring two local bands to open. Then we would need a headlining artist that we would need to book as soon as possible to get promotion rolling. We would also host a smaller, unplugged stage in a quieter, more relaxed environment to showcase some other local artists. We had a good plan, but who were these artists? And who else would help us facilitate such a big event?

The Youth Network became a significant connection for people and resources. There were lots of people throughout our community churches who were either artists willing to use their gifts or volunteers willing to serve in the background. And, of course, the Network had key leaders willing to promote the event and gather students to attend. Most importantly, one of the youth directors used to work at a Christian radio station and still had some connections. He began working toward booking the headlining artist for the main stage.

He was able to connect with an amazing Christian hip-hop and hard rock artist named Chris Greenwood, also known as "Manafest." We knew he was a huge pull for our youth culture because he had traveled north for Fusion a couple of years previous. We knew that he could provide a clear Gospel presentation as well as perform music that students would enjoy. We had all witnessed the result of his ministry and knew he was a good choice. The details were that we could book Manafest with his DJ or with his entire band. We really wanted the whole package, but it would cost us. This was a big component of the *how* that seemed difficult for us to wrap our minds around.

Nevertheless, God provided incredibly! We soon realized that the Spirit was moving in the hearts of our local churches with a desire to support this event. Even greater was the amount of unchurched community members thrilled to invest in an event for students. If you've ever lived in a smaller community, you know the tension of youth not having enough recreational options to keep them busy. Too often, boredom leads to trouble in small towns. Many parents, uncles, and aunts have lived this reality, and they're willing to invest in an alternative for their teens. So, when a group hosts an event for youth with a positive message, even if it's a Christian one, it often resonates with them. They realize the importance and long-standing rewards of community youth leaders building relationships with their teens. It didn't take much for them to be convinced that Epic Win might be a starting point for something great in the hearts and minds of Kenai Peninsula youth.

We managed to book Manafest and his band. We also had a variety of local artists on both stages with sounds ranging from metal to folk. The financial cost and volunteer effort were significant. However, we saw hundreds of students attend, many of whom would never attend our local churches. We saw students from our community who we knew did not have a relationship with Jesus. Many teens heard the Gospel for the first time that night. Some of them responded and were brought into our youth groups to develop lasting relationships and ongoing discipleship. That was all worth it—an Epic Win!

I'M SOLD ON COLLABORATION

I think I have always been sold out for collaboration, but my service with the Kenai Peninsula Youth Network definitely solidified it. Since then, I have tried to connect with any local network or ministerial. I've witnessed numerous collaborative efforts in the North, bringing small-town churches together for greater Gospel rewards. I believe it's a heart condition that stems from Jesus' first call to reach the world in Acts chapter one. We cling to our calling to be His "witnesses in Jerusalem" (our hometown). Conversely, when we struggle getting to "all Judea and Samaria" (our distance communities), we can create ways to bring those communities to us (Acts 1:8). The goal is to bring the Good News of Jesus to as many people as possible, using whatever collaborative methods we can to achieve that goal. In my experience, some of these methods have resulted in an overall cultural impact, bringing the conversation about Jesus to the forefront of the community. Others have had very specific impact on a certain individual brought to a crossroads in their life.

BRINGING HOPE TO THE NORTH

I mentioned earlier the revivals of days gone by. It's hard to keep the name Billy Graham separated from the word *revival*, as he hosted thousands over his lifetime, seeing hundreds of thousands of people respond and accept Christ. His son, Franklin, and grandson, Will, have carried on hosting these types of events, although under different names, each with a different flavor.

A few years ago, once I was established in my current role in the Yukon, The Billy Graham Association chose Whitehorse for one of their events. As the story goes, Will Graham was on a plane traveling to Anchorage, Alaska. Due to mechanical problems, they landed in Whitehorse. After spending a few days in the community, he felt Christ leading him to host one of his outreach events here. He contacted his Canadian team, and plans began to unfold for a "Celebration of Hope" with Will Graham.

I was impressed that they were not a fly-in-and-take-over outfit. The beginning stages were all centered around the local church, connecting with local pastors and ministry staff. It was exciting to be a part of their team, walking through the process to plan and facilitate such a large-scale event. It was really exciting to see the Gospel impact unfold before the event ever took place.

As I mentioned earlier, large, collaborative events spark conversation in the culture. As word got out that The Billy Graham Association was going to host an event in Whitehorse, there was kickback from atheist and agnostic groups. Some of them wrote in to the *Whitehorse Star* and *Yukon News* lashing out at the city for allowing such an event. We soon found out that even bad news can be good news. It primed the pump, leading to great conversations around the community, promoting the event to skeptics who would have otherwise ignored it. It also displayed great unity for the churches, as people discovered multiple denominations working together for this massive project. Our collaboration became a witnessing opportunity.

Then the event began, which was actually a few events back-to-back on a single weekend to give multiple opportunities for people to attend. All of them were hosted in the Air North hanger, "Yukon's Airline," which seemed to add to the intrigue and impact. People traveled from all over the Yukon and even from communities in the Northwest Territories. As would be expected, it was top-notch! Incredible musicians performed, and Will Graham gave an excellent message with a clear Gospel invitation. As we prayed for and anticipated, there were many people who were at a crossroads in their life and who accepted Jesus that weekend. Many lives were transformed because of our collaborative effort.

The most miraculous and perhaps mysterious accounts are witnessed at the end of longer stories, where God has been drawing someone to Himself over many years. And all of a sudden, everything connects in that moment, during a collaborative project or event. Not until after the event do we see the strategic Gospel touchpoints in that person's life. One such account came to fruition at that "Celebration of Hope" event.

A YOUNG WIDOW FINDS JESUS

Whitney is a Northern girl through and through, loves the wilderness, and can handle the wild when she needs to. One social media photo sticks out in my mind when I think of her. She's propped over a black bear with a rifle in her hand and her daughters by her side. They had spotted it from the roadside and decided to take it. Like I said, she can handle the wilds of the Yukon!

Growing up in a more legalistic Christian environment, Whitney's faith was never rooted in Jesus, although some seeds of truth were planted. This is often the case for many teens and young adults who attend these types of churches. The rules to be followed become more important than the Gospel to be preached. For Whitney, although faith and prayer were important, church and Jesus were not a priority and fell by the wayside as life continued on.

Soon, she met a young outdoorsman named Tanner, fell in love, and poured all their time into exploring the wilderness together. Faith was still a distant sidenote for Whitney, though not in a central focus. Eventually, they had a little girl. Not long after, Whitney was pregnant with their second. That's when tragedy struck. In a strange series of events, Whitney's husband was murdered. Out of a tragic scenario that no one could have seen coming, a young woman was left with two little girls to raise on her own.

Immediately after this horrific event, someone brought her story to our local church. Without hesitation, some of the congregation started to prepare and provide meals for Whitney and her family. It was a simple endeavor for our congregation but a blessing to those in mourning. Moreover, it became a significant Gospel seed sewn into Whitney's life.

Whitney was part of the crowd at one of Will Graham's "Celebration of Hope" events. She heard the clear Gospel message and responded. She walked to the front, received counsel and prayer, and fully submitted her life to Jesus. The counselor asked her, "What church did you come here with? Who invited you?" This question pointed to the typical scenario—that a local church canvassed and promoted the event to certain neighborhoods or that a certain person, connected to a local church, invited their friend or neighbor. Almost always, there was a connection that would give The Billy Graham Association a church contact who could follow up with the person who had accepted Christ so that their discipleship could continue.

This was not the case for Whitney, though. She had come on her own, seemingly by her own decision, but, in fact, under the Holy Spirit's guidance to this miraculous, life-changing encounter. Just then, she remembered the name of a certain church from years past. One that had provided for her and her family in their time of need. She realized that she did have a church connection. Although many might not remember her, God knew where she was headed the whole time. The Father had been establishing her discipleship before she had ever accepted the Son. How faithful is our God? How miraculous His salvation plan?

Diving a bit deeper into the spiritual realm, Whitney's story brings to mind the author of Hebrews, who wrote, "Are they not all ministering spirits sent out to serve for the sake of those who are to inherit salvation" (Heb. 1:14). How many angels were sent to care for Whitney and her daughters during those years of mourning and searching? How many instances did the enemy try to darken her world and try to hinder the plan that was playing out in the unseen world?

I have watched Whitney grow in leaps and bounds, ever aware of Christ's place in her life. In person and on social media, I have witnessed that she is not ashamed of the Gospel that has transformed her life. She openly proclaims a constant relationship with her Savior, revealing to the world what she is learning during daily devotions with Him. In the past couple of years, God has given Whitney the gift of falling in love once again to an outdoorsman named Lorne. He is a good man, accepting the two girls as his own, and they now have a third child.

This family will be transformed for generations to come. What began in the heart of a young widow will continue in the hearts of these three little girls. May they also accept Jesus and embrace Him with the same passion as their mother. May they find a church that places the Gospel in such high priority that they collaborate to evangelize. May their efforts increase the Lord's reach into searching hearts just like Whitney's.

THE PUSHBACK AND POST-PANDEMIC REALITY

The pushback against collaboration for big Gospel events is that evangelism needs to be relational, the person-to-person witness. I agree with this position on some level. I think sharing the Gospel individually is the most effective. However, I also think it's a both/and effort. If someone is called to put together a larger outreach effort during a particular community event or season, should they be dismissed? What if the Holy Spirit has guided them to something really important, part of the greater Gospel plan for that community? Or perhaps, like we outlined in Whitney's story, part of a greater plan for an individual? We should be asking, how we can help their vision come to fruition. How can we help them staff and fund the event? Where will the volunteers come from, and who directs them?

I'll say it again, this is where I have witnessed the incredible collaborative effort of Northern community churches. These smaller churches have learned to work together in order to fulfill their Gospel mandate. And in my experience, much of the pushback against collaborative events stems more from an emotional response than logical—or more appropriately stated, theological—positions. I get it; social media feeds are full of stories about large churches in urban centers pulling off incredible outreach projects and evangelism efforts. It can make the efforts of a small-town church feel insignificant. How can a church of twenty-five or fifty compete with that? The answer is simply to humbly collaborate.

Now, there is a second pushback in our post-pandemic world. Once large gatherings were limited, even mega-churches were having to think small-church. That is, until much of our ministries went online. Large churches started pumping out incredibly produced services and unique ways of gathering the Church. Many small-town church attenders could attend a larger church with better production, all from the comfort of their living room. Once again, the little guy felt a bit left out. And believe me, Northern churches felt that hit big time with a single internet provider that doesn't always provide the best options or connectivity. In all honesty, as I type these words, we're still trying to figure it out.

COLLABORATING YOUR EPIC WIN

Whether or not everything goes back to the way it was doesn't negate the original concept. Collaboration in person or online will always increase our reach. We all have been given specific skills and abilities; pastors and ministers have been called to specific congregations in specific communities. I am convinced that if we're lacking in any capacity, collaboration for the sake of the Gospel will always receive God's blessing. Moreover, the Body of Christ will rise up and rally behind these types of efforts.

Starting today, let's not let the size of our church or community stop us from dreaming. Let's not allow larger churches to determine what we can or can't achieve. Let's not let COVID-19, or whatever flu virus might shut us down next, prevent us from creating something new. Whatever Epic Win we envision, let's tell people about it and gather them to it. Let's ask them to partner with us, pray with us, dream and create with us. Let's keep collaborating to bring the Good News of Jesus Christ to the forefront of our ministries, our churches, and our communities.

CHAPTER EIGHT

MINISTRY IS A TEAM SPORT: KEY PLAYERS

"Therefore, my beloved brothers, be steadfast, immovable, always abounding in the work of the Lord, knowing that in the Lord your labor is not in vain."

1 Corinthians 15:58

A few years ago, I had the opportunity to attend a church planting conference. It was a great interdenominational experience, networking with pastors and church leaders from a wide variety of networks and fellowships. Overall, it was a great experience! I would suggest that all church leaders get out of their theological camp once in a while to focus on the big picture of what God might be calling the Church to achieve nationally or even globally.

That being said, hosting and attending these types of interdenominational events carry a bit of risk. One must be acutely aware of the theological and philosophical diversity that will be packed into that conference room. I experienced this tension at that church planting conference—specifically, an aggression toward a particular leadership position. One of the speakers, who, according to the program, was scheduled to speak on church growth metrics in a post-Christian culture, threw us all a curveball.

He was (and still is) a brilliant individual and an expert in the field of church growth trends and data. I was really looking forward to the session. All of a sudden, mid-talk, he shifted. In an intense and condescending tone, he began calling out any churches who were not willing to place women in equal positions of leadership as men. He actually ended his talk camping on that issue, stating, "The game is too difficult to not be playing with a full roster." It was a clear shaming of any churches who are metaphorically leaving women on the bench. What happened next was really interesting.

A third of the people cheered. A third sat unaffected. And a third shook their heads, muttering under their breaths, looking down at their notes awkwardly. *This issue is not so cut and dry,* I thought to myself. He had started his talk with such excellent content and passion. His research had the potential to unify denominations toward common goals and objectives. Then almost randomly, he used his platform to address a ministry leadership pet-peeve. There was an assumption in his voice that the topic of women in leadership is a trivial one. He ignored the interdenominational setting we were in, with numerous backgrounds and traditions. He ignored the overall intent of the conference, which was to unify in order to plant more churches and reach more people with the Gospel. He ignored that we were striving for Christ's prayer "that they may all be one, just as you, Father, are in me, and I in you, that they also may be in us, so that the world may believe that you have sent me" (John 17:21). His plan was not very well thought-out.

A couple of years later, I was sitting around a table with a consulting team. We had been assembled to assess a traditional church in a small town and give them some insight on how they might see revitalization. The topic of women in leadership came up. I remarked that in this church setting, it would be a huge decision for them, one that would take some time. Eyes rolled.

"Are we still talking about this?" one of them asked.

There's that assumption again, I thought to myself. *Why do we keep treating women in leadership as a trivial decision?*

WOMEN IN LEADERSHIP

Some of you are questioning why I'm even writing about this. You may even be tempted to check the publishing date, to see if this was a rewrite of some 1965 ministry resource. I'll save you the time; it's not. In truth, for many churches all over Western society (never mind in the developing world), this is completely a current issue that still needs to be a part of the conversation.

Before I tell you what I might be against, let me highlight what I'm for. I'm for women being placed into leadership positions. In chapter five, you may have taken note that both my coach and assistant captain were women. That being said, for some of you (men and women), reading about women in leadership in chapter five made you a little uncomfortable. Believe it or not, I'm for you as well! I understand the context. I understand the conviction. I understand the tension. If you're from a smaller community, especially in a conservative culture, you know what I'm talking about. For you, the struggle is real. For you, it's not an easy decision for your church. Convictions and culture have placed you on a different journey. One that takes time. One that includes lots of discussion and patience, Scriptural study and prayer. I've had to navigate the complexities of building a co-ed team without allowing the pressure—or worse, ridicule—hinder where the Spirit is leading the ministry.

BUILDING A CO-ED TEAM

The idea of female leadership in the church was not something that came easily for me. I grew up in an evangelical Baptist church that was sometimes more Baptist than evangelical, if you know what I mean. There were conservative viewpoints regarding women that I accepted as absolutes. Men gathered around boardroom tables without a woman's perspective brought into the discussion. Male church leaders shepherded women without female insight or involvement. This was centered around culture, not condescension.

At present, I am still under the personal Scriptural conviction that male oversight within the family as husband and father (Eph. 5:22-33; Col. 3:18-24; 1 Peter 3:1-7) and male oversight within the Church as pastor and elder (Titus 1:5-9; 1 Tim. 3:1-7; 1 Peter 5:1-4) are the most beneficial leadership structures. I understand that this comes from my conservative, more literal approach to

New Testament passages. Conversely, I am no longer under the conviction that every leadership position in the church must be held by men. Quite the opposite. After a long process of discovery and debate (with God and others), I've come to the conviction that this isn't exactly how Jesus intended His Church to function. Pointing again back to chapter five, those two amazing leaders were key players in God's plan to shape my viewpoints on what co-ed leadership might look like.

Carmen and Morgan showed me that ministry can be a co-ed sport and that an effective leader should seek to build a co-ed team, even in a Northern culture, where conservative values and traditions run high and where these conversations can be sensitive, if not heated. Within this type of environment, I would suggest that building a co-ed leadership team needs to be established with tact. While on my journey to embrace female leadership in the church, the Lord showed me some of the unique benefits that can come from obtaining a co-ed ministry team. I'd like to unpack some of where God has led me with the chance that He might provide some guide-points for your journey.

PRIVATE MEETINGS

Many a male ministry leader has fallen victim to an array of problems in this arena. He decided to meet with and discuss sensitive topics with a female staff member, ministry volunteer, or congregate without the safeguards of accountability over the meeting. One does not have to travel too far to hear tragic stories of this practice ending with difficult results. There is a better way.

It's not uncommon for the male leader to call in a female leader during the meeting. I have benefited from this practice throughout my ministry career, specifically related to my first pastoral position in youth ministry. There were numerous occasions of female teenagers wanting to meet with or speak to me in private. When an issue arose, I would ask Carmen or Morgan to sit in and help me navigate the problem. Though it wasn't always an option,

I tried to give them as much lead time as possible. Having them as a second was paramount to achieving the desired and God-honoring outcomes.

The addition of a female leader brought about protection for the teen, protection for me as the pastor, and protection for the church as a whole. Accountability is an amazing protector! As another option, I have known other male pastors who bring their wives into private meetings with women. Either option provides a level of relatability from a female standpoint, but more importantly, it provides that protective accountability piece.

Now that I have a bit more experience, I'm convinced that there's an even better way. Why do I have to be in the room at all? Having key players who are women working directly with women is a far more beneficial experience. Objectively, the female leader (like any male leader) should at least be qualified on some level and have the proven character to be coaching and mentoring. Furthermore, having some type of informal reporting in place will keep everything above-board. All of this, of course, is assuming you have female leaders who have been identified, trained, and empowered to lead in such a capacity.

I fully understand that smaller churches typically have limited personnel. It takes a shift in priorities and maybe even a shift in culture. If this standard is set in place, I believe that very early on in the process, comfortable, healthy relationships will be created and deepened. I assure you that the individuals, the leadership, and the church as a whole will benefit.

FEMALE ROLE MODELS

Within the local church, who will young women gifted in leadership become? Who can they look up to? What can they aspire to be? Will they be forced to look outside the church for role models? In building a co-ed ministry team, role-modeling needs to be a part of the conversation. This has already shifted in many churches, especially in large urban centers; but in many smaller communities, they're still working through the process.

With great success, I have seen women take on incredible ministry projects as the key point-person, organizing teams to meet church and community needs. I've personally experienced the amazing work that can be done through female counselors, as you'll find out in a later chapter. And let's be honest with ourselves. How many of our women, who have been called into missions, end up serving in major missionary roles? In many cases, these women carry more leadership responsibility than the supporting male church leaders serving back at home.

What about preaching and teaching? Yup, I went there! This is a tough one for smaller, conservative contexts. I have personally had to journey through this question. Are we adequately providing an arena for women to share what they've experienced? Do they have an opportunity to communicate what God is revealing to them? How, when, and where can they share their stories with us? I have witnessed women who teach the Word with great clarity and humility, not with an axe to grind, but as valuable accountants of God's greatness and goodness. As they've shared and explained how God has moved in their lives, I have received some significantly different perspectives that I never would have gained from a male speaker or teacher.

I understand that these words may be difficult for some. I started this conversation knowing the massive culture shift for some churches to begin promoting women in leadership. In the traditional sense, many women who lead and teach still have husbands and children. I have listened to enough female leaders to know that this often becomes a tension point. Balancing the call to be a wife and mother with the call to lead and teach must be difficult to navigate in and of itself without the addition of external voices. Yet I have to admit that the work these women do and the roles they carry inside and outside of the home give them unique experiences that increase their leadership potential.

For those of us in the context of smaller churches and ministries, we have limitations as to the number of qualified people around us. Wouldn't it be tragic to rule out a qualified female leader just to appease a tradition or cultural status quo? I'm suggesting that if we have women in our churches whose character, integrity, and gifting are in the right place, could we not at least begin the discussion on having them serve in leadership? Could we not consider the benefits for young women in our youth groups and college ministries, giving them someone to connect with and, perhaps, aspire to be like. I believe that with tact and grace, we can and should bring the discussion forward.

THE FIRST-STRING

Getting back to our team analogy, a first string is often considered the key players on any given team. They're put on the field immediately after the coin toss. The idea isn't based on a few regular players and a couple of superstars, but instead, a grouping of players, each excelling at their individual roles while working together as a team. This grouping of key players will give a team the best chance of an early lead and, hopefully, a win.

So, what makes a first string in the ministry game? In sports, it might be a natural talent or specific ability. In the ministry game, however, I have witnessed that consistency and integrity have proven to be far more valuable than any other skill or aptitude. Throughout my ministry in the North, I have been blessed with amazing first-string players, both in Alaska and the Yukon. They've never been a huge team of people, but they have proven to have incredible consistency and integrity both in their personal lives and in their ministry service. Even with a great coach and a great assistant captain, a ministry's success launches out from these first-string players. They adjust schedules, gather resources, and focus on their spiritual health to serve faithfully. Once systems and structures are in place, first-string players can often carry the ministry forward, even when the key leader is absent. Pastors and church leaders in small communities should be seeking out people like this, a first-string who carry these two vital character traits.

PLAYERS OF CONSISTENCY

What does a consistent player look like? Many ministries have those occasional helpers that assist with donating items or putting some time into a special event or fundraiser. Don't get me wrong, these folks who accomplish the "odd jobs" of ministry are essential to the greater plan of the church. I don't discount their service in the slightest! That being said, these players are typically not your first-string. They love serving, but they'll likely never have the consistency to keep serving week in and week out. Especially when ministry gets tough.

In Paul's first letter to the Corinthian church, we get an idea of what people of consistency look like. "Therefore, my beloved brothers, be steadfast, immovable, always abounding in the work of the Lord, knowing that in the Lord your labor is not in vain" (1 Cor. 15:58). The operative word is "abounding." A ministry's first-string needs to be made up of people who truly want to be there—people who have a deep concern for the lost and a deep enjoyment for the ministry. More than likely, these are the people who were keeping the ministry afloat before we ever arrived and before anyone was ever hired to do the job.

A first-string doesn't show up just to put in their Christian-service time. A first-string doesn't show up because they felt some guilted obligation. These key players can't wait to show up for anything and everything. For meetings, functions, and events, they often show up when you do. Sometimes, they show up before you do, waiting in the parking lot for the doors to open. Once in the mix of things, they get to work with a joyful heart without being rallied to do so. These players are motivated beyond what is considered normal. These players are fully engaged in the work of the Lord. These key players are your consistent first-string.

PLAYERS OF INTEGRITY

Next, we should seek out players who possess integrity. Consistency may come easy for our first-string players because they're passionate about the ministry, but it's just good works without a strong personal relationship with Christ. King Solomon said it best: "Keep your heart with all vigilance, for from it flow the springs of life" (Prov. 4:23). Our service should not stem from a passion for ministry but from an intimate passion for Jesus Christ. What we value and cherish in our hearts will be evident in our ministry. As ministry leaders, it's a given that we should follow Scripture and daily seek God's plan for our lives. If we're not doing this, forget about ever coaching the first-string team. Our lives must show a passion for Christ and a consistent movement toward Christ-like character.

For those serving as our first-string, we will see the condition of their heart through their service. They, too, should be men and women who raise the bar of Christ-like character. They should be people who know and stand firm on Scripture—not just while working within some ministry area, but as a standard for their lives. These first-string players are our core people, who hold a lot of leadership value. In turn, they should carry equal amounts of personal responsibility, not just for their words and actions, but also for their spiritual well-being and the condition of their heart.

SECOND AND THIRD STRING PLAYERS

Although Scripture outlines a high standard for all believers, we'd be wise to tread lightly when holding ministry volunteers to the highest standard. Remember that the above paragraphs were focused on our first-string players. In my experience, only those within that first-string should be held to the high level of consistency and integrity previously outlined. With the second and third-string volunteers and what I would refer to as occasional players, we should be cautious in how much we expect from them. Even though their consistency and integrity aren't at the highest level, these players are still essential. Never underestimate their service. There is so much value in their occasional duties of the ministry, which lighten the load of first-string players and coaches and captains.

Our second and third strings need to hear and feel our appreciation. We should focus on building relationships with these ministry workers, leaving room for the Holy Spirit to work on the hearts for service. When the time is right, our relational investment and the leading from the Spirit will bring them to future opportunities for accountability, challenge, and potential spots on the first-string line-up. We should rest in knowing that the right key players will rise to the surface at the right time according to God's plan.

BUILDING A HEALTHY TEAM

The standard of consistency and integrity should be fairly easy to spot within your team's behavior. If a player is struggling within the team, they're often struggling in their walk with Jesus. Still not sure? Try asking yourself a few of the following questions:

- Do you have players who frequently act selfishly with others?
- Do you have players who have been caught in half-truths to see their opinions heard or their plans fulfilled?
- Do you have players who spend more time talking about what the team needs to do instead of what God will do within the team?
- Do you have players who tend to act like the work of their ministry area takes precedence over the greater mission of the church?

Steadfast consistency and integrity within one's behavior will more times than not show a team member with a healthy heart, keeping in mind that just like us, all of our players will make mistakes and go through times of struggle. With grace, we should focus on whether or not our team members have any inconsistent or potentially damaging patterns in their lives. By building our team up, challenging them to be consistent, and holding them to a standard of integrity both in their area of service and personal walk with Jesus, we'll be on our way to building a healthy team of key players.

CHAPTER NINE

MOOSE MEAT RECOVERY

"As you sent me into the world, so I have sent them into the world."

John 17:18

In days gone by, definitely pre-internet, culture and mindsets were solely centered around their local community. Big city newspapers with big city stories ended up being more of an exciting read than a true sign of real life or things to come. People tended to cling to long-time traditions and a familiar way of life. The thought of new ideas and new ways seemed distant and unrealistic. Those were the days when travel and communication were limited. The world was massive, and there was a sense of security within a small community. If we're to be honest with ourselves, it sounds attractive doesn't it? For those who have lived long enough, it sounds nostalgic.

We who live in small communities try really hard to keep this cultural narrative going. We want to ignore that the internet has brought urban life and culture into every one of our homes, and into every one of our pockets through mobile devices. We don't want to believe that at some point in the past few decades, the outside world showed up at our front door, and we somehow signed a life-time lease. We want to believe in the simpler life, and yet we're still checking our cell phones constantly. And we're still spending way too many evenings with streaming services. In many ways, it's true there are significant differences to small-town life. Nevertheless, we'd be wise not to let it become a foothold for pride, pretending that we're *nothing* like the rest of the world.

In my experience, many small community churches haven't just tried to keep the nostalgia going, they've got a death-grip on it. In this type of church culture, clinging to tradition and the familiar way of doing things has become their identifier and something of which to be proud. Despite the changes in the community around them, these local churches have hit the pause button at some point. As the surrounding community changed, a fear of the outside world set in. The distinctives of old-ways-gone-by have eventually become as foundational as Scripture. The identity of the congregation becomes so wrapped up in *how* they do church that the *why* has been forgotten.

Church leaders in this type of culture might try to defend their position and culture by quoting the popular "Christianese" phrase, "We are in the world but not of the world!" It doesn't add up, though, because it promotes legalism and isolation. Although their actual church building is physically in this world, the people have definitely pulled themselves completely out of it. They have missed the context and intent behind the prayer that popularized the phrase. Found in John 17, Jesus, speaking to His Father on our behalf, said, "I do not ask that you take them out of the world, but that you keep them from the evil one. They are not of the world, just as I am not of the world . . . As you sent me into the world, so I have sent them into the world" (John 17:15-16, 18).

Many followers of Christ living in smaller communities battle against this cultural mindset on a regular basis. Somehow, we must find a way to encourage our local churches to cling to the heart behind Christ's prayer, to remain contextual in bringing His Gospel to the culture we've been called to reach. It's never easy, and we should be cautious in our steps toward bringing these churches into cultural relevance. If our desires are based in our personal preference, they will ultimately fail because we're adhering to a similar mindset, just with a different preferential twist.

It will most likely take some steps toward innovation and creativity. It will most definitely take some steps away from tradition and comfort. None of these steps are easy, but they carry us on a journey toward a true evangelical focus. The local church recaptures their love for and commitment to the Great Commission (Matt. 28:18-20). Gospel-driven projects and events are planned, meeting real needs while having authentic conversations and regularly sharing the Gospel. These local churches will have been gradually transformed into Christians who love reaching their local community and who have a tangible impact on their local culture.

REACHING THE LOCAL COMMUNITY

Like much of Western society, Alaska had its fair share of churches struggling to balance serving needs inside the church, while continuing evangelism efforts outside the church. As I interacted with local pastors and church leaders, we all had to guard against getting so focused on the internal church community that we neglected our call to reach the Kenai Peninsula. If we weren't careful, a club-like mentality could slip in and take over. The risk is neglecting our relationships with unchurched friends and acquaintances. This becomes a bad example for the local church and a terrible witness for our community.

Thankfully, Pastor Keith promoted a strong Gospel-centered balance to everyone who attended our church. Discipleship and evangelism are not separate endeavors, as some churches may knowingly or unknowingly teach and facilitate. Though the internal community of our local church was definitely important, it didn't end there. It was definitely matched with a strong outward focus. It was exciting to be a part of a serving and giving church culture, where the end goal was centered around seeing people come to know Christ. We had a couple of well-established ministries that specifically served our local community. More importantly, these ministries were not centered on traditional projects or programs. These were fresh, innovative ideas that addressed the needs of our Northern culture. They would build strong bridges into the community that led back to our church and ultimately to the Gospel.

First was our Moose Meat Recovery program, a true Northern outreach, run in cooperation with our men's ministry. Our church worked with local law enforcement to make sure that meat from large roadkill animals was not wasted. I realize that this may sound distasteful to those who are not accustomed to the process. I assure you that one moose can put meat on a family's table for months, if not all year. Day or night, our men would receive a call from a state trooper giving the location where the animal was killed. The men would meet the trooper, harvest the meat, package it, and place it in a freezer located in the church basement. Those people in our local community who might be struggling financially knew that they could stop by our church and put meat on their table that night. As they picked up their moose meat, we had opportunities to hear their stories, share the Gospel, and pray with them.

The second outward-focused ministry was started by two mothers in the church and had an incredible impact on our local community. They titled it Coats4Community. It was a simple idea addressing a tangible Northern need. There was a bin by our church office where people could drop off coats, snow pants, hats, gloves, etc. If someone came by the church and needed some winter gear, they were free to take a couple of items from the bin. When the bin was full, the items were taken to a storage unit. Then at the beginning of winter, our church hosted a Winter Gear Giveaway. Our auditorium would be covered in outdoor clothing items! Many people were warmer during those winter months because two mothers had a desire to positively impact our community, and our church had a desire to support their efforts. This, of course, does not include the dozens of Gospel conversations that took place during each pickup and giveaway events.

Pastor Keith didn't just promote outreach ministry within our church circles, he proved this balance in his own life as well. He wasn't known for sitting in his study all day preparing sermons. He was community-minded, and it wasn't uncommon to see him in Coffee Roasters or another coffee shop meeting with people from our church or the community. More importantly, he served as a chaplain within our community EMS department. He interacted with the unbelieving world on a daily basis. Now that I have moved on to other ministry opportunities, I realize how much I under-appreciated his role and his ministry philosophy. Keith encouraged us to get involved in the local community as part of our calling to ministry. It was never just about church folk.

Taking Keith's philosophy—or should I say, theology—to heart, I started looking for opportunities to connect with people outside the church. As a youth pastor, I was able to use my gifts in the local schools instead of just focusing on our churched teens. It's not that I neglected our regular students, but this helped me bring discipleship and evangelism into a single focus.

MENTORSHIP EVANGELISM

One particular area of service that gave me great fulfilment was within a mentorship program based in a local middle school. As a mentor, I was given the opportunity to spend time with students who were having some struggles. The academic needs often stemmed from behavioral problems. Because the mentors were not parents or teachers, it gave us a unique opportunity to speak into their lives and to hear what was really going on. Unfortunately, these struggles in school were too often the outcome of rough home lives and dysfunctional family relationships. It was a privilege to serve in this role, but a tough one, nonetheless.

I'll never forget my first official meeting with the three junior high boys whom I would be mentoring. Within the introductions and the getting-to-know-each-other conversation, I found out about their parents and families. One twelve-year-old boy told me that he lived in a trailer with his parents and older brother. Sometimes, they'd all be gone for days at a time. The second boy added, "And they don't ever leave him any food!" I then found out that it was not uncommon to have mustard or ketchup sandwiches or other condiment-based meals. All of sudden, he perked up. "But there's a Chinese family who lives a couple of trailers down. Sometimes, they invite me over. Their food is awesome!" It was very clear that he was not making up this stuff.

With such poor nutrition, there were plausible reasons for his struggles with learning and behavior-correction. Thankfully, the other two boys were fed better than the first, but they had other challenging family situations. The more I got to know these boys, the more my heart ached for them. I had to walk a crooked line between listening to their disturbing tales of homelife, yet trying to encourage them to press forward. I had to balance keeping family secrets, yet being obligated to report abuse and neglect when it came to my knowledge. Even during the latter, when I had to force them to have tough conversations with counseling faculty, they trusted me. They listened to every bit of encouragement and counsel I gave them. Over time, I developed great relationships with these young men.

Unfortunately, as is the case in most public schools, I could not openly evangelize. However, I was able to focus on a biblical principle without quoting Scripture to speak into their lives (i.e., "Do unto others, as you would have them do unto you"—Matt. 7:12). I could also invite them to attend any youth event or activity that our church was putting on in the evenings or weekends. Eventually, they started attending the youth program at our church from time to time. This gave me full opportunity to tell them about Jesus.

Serving at the center of unchurched culture keeps us well-seasoned as ministry workers. By daily connecting with the outside world, we witness the harsh realization that so many people are facing an eternity in Hell. We are, therefore, to provide the Gospel bridge as an alternative outcome. With sadness, I cannot say any of these three boys made a decision to follow Jesus. Nevertheless, they definitely heard the Gospel a number of times. I can only trust and pray that God has added water to the seeds He allowed me to plant in their lives.

COUCH-SURFING CRISIS

On the Kenai Peninsula, it's rare to find a homeless person wandering around. This doesn't mean that our part of Alaska was immune to homelessness. There are a few shelters, but many of the Peninsula's homeless tend to couch-surf, live in vehicles, or put up a tent in the woods on the outskirts of town. If they truly must live on the street, they often find their way to Anchorage, where the population is higher and there's an established downtown core.

A few times each month, I would help out a local non-profit that helped at-risk youth find employment. Through this organization, I heard that there were many teens in our area who were also couch-surfing, living in vehicles, or residing in tents. Soon enough, I found myself in a meeting with the school board's homeless teen liaison. She explained that there were over one hundred teens registered as homeless within her program. These students were committed to attending school and, in turn, received breakfast and lunch during the school year. This provided some preventive measures against the teens skipping school altogether. Now, perhaps you're wondering, "What about when school is closed?"

Throughout the summer months, they got by fairly well. With the Northern midnight sun bringing long days, warm weather, and high tourism traffic, there seemed to be ample opportunity for them to fend for themselves. However, Christmas was a different story. During the Christmas break, the teens faced some harsh challenges. Not only did they have to find food for two weeks, but they also had to find shelter in Alaska in December when it is cold and dark. Not to mention the psychological ramifications that came from being homeless during the holiday season when portraits of family get-togethers are promoted everywhere. These teens were part of our community; something had to be done!

It was nearing the end of November, just under a month before Christmas. It would be a challenge, but Pastor Keith was more than on-board. We felt a buzz of excitement that can only come from taking on a Gospel-driven challenge like this. That Sunday, we put a call out to the congregation. We were going to aim for 130 boxes to provide one for each teen under the liaison's care, as well as a few extras. We gave each attender a list of non-perishable items to be placed into a box roughly the size of an apple box (twenty feet by twelve feet by eight feet). The sizing guidelines would provide easier transport and prevent jealousy amongst the other teens. And as per the liaison's instructions, the box must be able to close.

Gifts and winter clothing items were acceptable to fill any empty space that wasn't filled with food. Furthermore, cards and notes were allowed as long as no personal information was given, and no cash or checks were permitted. Once filled, each box would be dropped off at the church office one week before the start of Christmas break. This way, the liaison would have the time needed to distribute the boxes before the school closed.

Within a few days, the boxes started mounting up in the hallway outside the church office. The congregation was more than enthusiastic about answering the rally cry. My role from that point was content control. As a box came in, I would open it and check that all food items were intact and non-perishable. Secondly, I would open any envelopes, scanning notes and cards for personal information and removing any cash or check, as per the liaison's request. Any monetary gifts were placed into our youth outreach fund to be used for other projects. Although this was explained to the congregation beforehand, sometimes our hearts prevent us from hearing the details, and that's okay. Lastly, I would make sure the box was packed neatly enough to be closed securely.

By the end of the first week, our quota was half-filled. Small groups were hosting box-filling parties, adding even more boxes outside of what their households were already providing. Then word started to spread. I noticed that some of the boxes were being dropped off by people who didn't attend our church. It turned out that some of our attenders took a few box lists and handed them to friends, family, and coworkers. I called the homeless teen liaison at the end of the first week to let her know what was happening. She was thrilled!

"But what am I going to do with all the extra boxes?" she asked.

"We might actually have to cut people off from giving," I replied.

Sure enough, by the following Sunday, I had an announcement to make.

"Thank you so much for your generosity! Though we're just under one hundred homeless teen boxes, I see that some of you have brought your boxes today. And we know that there will be a number of boxes arriving within the next few days. Please keep in mind that we still have to transport all these boxes to the schools for distribution by the end of this week."

Looking at the number of boxes, I wasn't looking forward to the multiple trips in my little SUV to deliver them. I was definitely going to need some help! Thankfully, when God moves people within a project like this, transportation is a minor detail for Him. The owner of the local glass shop attended our church. He approached me after the service.

"Need any help transporting those boxes?"

"Do I?" I responded. "Absolutely! What do you have in mind?"

Soon enough, we arranged for a pickup that week with their cube van with more than enough room to transport all the boxes in one trip! The day came, and their employees and I got every box loaded. The homeless teen liaison had arranged a large storage space at the local middle school. It was central in the community, making it great for distribution. I knew that there would be a few more to arrive in the next couple of days, but I could manage those in my personal vehicle.

As schools closed that week, all of the liaison's homeless teens received an incredible gift for Christmas. The extra boxes were given to a few connected families who she knew were struggling. And because I read every note and card, I know that almost every person received an even greater gift. Those cards and notes held well-worded encouragements and Gospel invitations. Much like the boys I mentored, I can't validate that any of those homeless teens accepted Christ. I rest in knowing that we answered our call to care for the needs of others and plant seeds of salvation along the way.

CONNECTING WITH THE WORLD

There are numerous ways that a local church, regardless of its size, can connect with their community. Unfortunately, too often, it's easier to stay inwardly focused, choosing to camp on a version of discipleship that has removed evangelism, which is necessary to keep disciples making disciples. Sure, we may beef up our missions giving and pat ourselves on the back as we take care for some community need. And I'm not saying that missionaries don't need our support or that tangible needs shouldn't be met. I'm just saying that if the extent of our outreach is giving and serving without actually entering into conversation and actually sharing the Gospel, there's a massive piece missing from our outreach.

What about your community? What do they need? What do they want? How can your local church provide something for them with the goal of reaching them with the Good News of Jesus? Perhaps it's time to start booking some lunch appointments and coffee meetings with non-profit and community outreach leaders. Spend time in diners, coffee shops, and other local establishments having conversations with management and staff about what they're seeing as community problems and issues.

Maybe it's time to canvas a couple neighborhoods, simply asking them what their greatest need is. Don't just take a shot-in-the-dark approach to your outreach. Take the necessary steps to educate yourself about your community and the challenges it faces. Keep a watchful eye on local news stories and social media feeds surrounding your community. Better still, actually have conversations with people in *your* neighborhood. Gather as much information as possible.

Lastly, don't just settled for what's been done in the past. Don't allow local church history to determine future ministry. Choose innovation over tradition. It might not be as crazy-sounding as Moose Meat Recovery, but it might be something just as unique and just as effective. Then you'll start seeing outreach plans unfold that are truly Gospel-driven, leaving seeds planted all over your community.

PART FOUR

HARDSHIP IN THE NORTH

CHAPTER TEN

I DON'T DO DEATH WELL

"Jesus wept. So the Jews said, 'See how he loved him!'"

John 11:35-36

Before moving to the North, my experiences with death had been few and far-between. Though I was almost thirty years of age, I had never actually been to a funeral or memorial service of any kind. When I was younger, a couple of family friends had passed away. The first was a teen with whom I was friends when we were preschool age. The second was a good friend of my parents, whom my brothers and I would call "aunt" when we were young kids. In both of these situations, I had fallen out of connection long before their passing. My only guess as to why I never experienced a state of mourning would be the distance of time, which also distanced the relationships in some way.

This lack of mourning was not just from distance of time but also physical distance. My grandmother had passed a few years before we moved to Alaska. I remember feeling somewhat guilty that I didn't feel more loss. And yet, she lived in England, and I grew up in Canada. And since then, all but one of my grandparents have also passed on. The absence of sorrow feels awkward. I definitely loved them and have some fond memories. There was always a card on my birthday, a quick call at Christmas, and every few years, a trip to see them. That being said, the relationship wasn't really built on much more than that. Even the visits always seemed quick and not really foundational moments for building strong relationships.

From a relational perspective, I just didn't have enough of a connection with any of these friends and family who have passed. Therefore, I didn't ever feel any authentic sense of mourning. After years of reflecting on this fact, I realize that although I was saved from the pain that sorrow brings, I was at a significant disadvantage. I did not learn how to fully process human death until I was well into adulthood.

LOSING A LOVED ONE

In the Gospel of John, we read that Jesus experienced loss. "Now when Mary came to where Jesus was and saw him, she fell at his feet, saying to him, 'Lord, if you had been here, my brother would not have died'" (John 11:32). Then, as Jesus approaches the tomb, He is overcome by emotion. "Jesus wept. So the Jews said, 'See how he loved him!'" (John 11:35-36). In response, Jesus prays to His Father, then performs an incredible miracle, raising His friend from the dead (John 11:41-43).

We don't get many details about the relationship that Jesus had with Lazarus. We struggle to understand why Jesus would experience such a significant loss if He was about to raise Lazarus from the dead. Conversely, we know that Jesus was not deceptive in nature or character. So, we are convinced by the emotion that Jesus displayed that He truly experienced authentic loss. In fact, we accept that the death of His friend Lazarus caused Him sorrow and a true time of mourning.

WHEN A COMMUNITY LOSES A CHILD

Almost a year after arriving in Alaska, a family in our church lost a young boy in a tragic accident involving livestock at the local fairgrounds. The Martin family grew up in our community and were very active in a variety of clubs and sports. Blair and Ronna Martin were dedicated members of our church family, often serving in leadership roles. It devastated our congregation and a good portion of the Kenai Peninsula as a whole. It was a horrific event, yet this type of tragedy showed the benefits of living in small communities. Everyone was interconnected, now rallying around the loss that had taken place—not just to get some news story, but to truly grieve with the family, knowing that a part of their community had been taken away too soon.

My wife and I were connected with this family in a number of ways, most significantly on a weekly basis through a small group Bible study. The young boy's name was Matti, a mischievous fella who could give anyone a good laugh with his antics. To our family, Matti was most known for his weekly request to sing "Jesus Loves Me" in our small group. Regardless of his rambunctious nature, he loved Jesus very much, enjoyed learning about Him, and of course, delighted in singing about Him.

I'll never forget the first time I walked into the Martins' home following this terrible event. Everything seemed to move in slow motion. Scanning the room, I saw friends and family members holding onto one another and weeping over their loss. It was a terrible experience to see so many people in such agonizing pain. It felt very much like the scene explained in John chapter eleven as Jesus surveys the crowd of people mourning the loss of Lazarus. For the first time in my life, I could relate to the emotions that Jesus felt that day, being "deeply moved in [my] spirit and greatly troubled" (John 11:33). Even today, every time I read that passage, I am taken back to that moment standing in the doorway of our friends' home.

Matti's father, Blair, approached me as I stood just inside the door. I had developed a good friendship with him over the past year not only through our small group, but also through our youth program, where he had two children, and as a lay leader in our church. Blair and I also met for coffee quite frequently. As he met me in the doorway, he embraced me in such a way that I had never experienced with anyone before. Normally standing more than a foot taller than me, I felt like I was holding his entire body weight on my shoulders. Blair squeezed me tightly, and I could feel his body shudder with each bitter sob. Every ounce of this typically confident and jovial man had been utterly defeated, save for the grace and Gospel of Jesus to which

Blair and his family held so tightly before and now during those dark days. It was on that day that I came face to face with mourning for the first time. I will never forget that moment.

Over the next week, friends and fellow believers cleared their schedules. It was our role to take time and mourn with the Martin family. Many prepared food and care packages for the family. Others helped with preparations for the memorial service in order to lighten the family's load of that painful work. My role was to prepare a slide show of photographs for the memorial service. We all did our part so that the Martins could work through the grief. We were called to use our gifts and abilities to assist this family in their time of mourning.

Many who experience the loss of child endure subsequent losses related to marriage, finance, parenting, and other family dynamics. I remember speaking to Blair a few months after the memorial as he explained this realty to me. With conviction, he determined, "This can't happen to Ronna and me!" Over the next few years, I watched this couple embrace Christ-centered counseling, drawing nearer to each other and their remaining children with more devotion and intentionality. I witnessed a submission to God's will on what could not be changed or brought back, leading them to a relationship with our Heavenly Father for which many Christians long. Of course, their healing has not removed the sorrow of losing Matti. It remains, as perhaps it should. Nevertheless, even that sorrow has been transformed into something amazing, using Matti's life as a launching pad for new opportunities, specifically, "connecting generations through agriculture and education" within a non-profit organization titled in his honor, "Matti's Farm" (*www.MattisFarm.org*).

CANCER

As indicated in the first few chapters, the church in Alaska to which I was called was located half an hour from where Nicole grew up. The church leadership had no idea that I had ever been to Alaska, never mind that we had family nearby living on the Kenai Peninsula. Obviously, living so close to

Nicole's family after being away for so long was an incredible blessing. The grandparents, Dale and Diane, were cherishing the time they got to spend with our son, Jude. When my father-in-law wasn't working, they would drive out in the middle of the day to spend time with him and Nicole. I would come home for lunch, and they'd all be enthralled with his antics. In fact, due to these frequent visits, they were able to see a lot of our son's firsts, including rolling over, getting new teeth, clapping his hands, and even taking his first steps. These midday visits became highlights in our week.

There was one lunch visit, however, that did not have the same jovial tone. Nicole's dad had been having some back problems over the past few months. His back had become very painful, keeping him from work and recreation. That day, he had just been to the hospital for some tests, and the plan was to have lunch with us before heading back home. We knew about the tests and were waiting to hear what the test results had revealed. Everyone wanted to find out what was wrong, so we could get Grandpa back in action.

Nothing ever prepares you for a loved one saying the word *cancer*—a word that floats around within our culture but becomes a very different word when it impacts your immediate family. At first, Dale didn't use the word. He said, "The doctor found a few spots on my lungs." This really didn't make any sense, since his back was the problem. As the conversation continued, we discovered that the spots were cancer, and they had been there for some time. Over time, the cancer had spread into his spinal cord. The pain in his back was due to a tumor separating his vertebrae. They had classed Grandpa at Stage 4. Unless aggressive treatment was administered, the cancer would continue to spread; the tumors would continue to grow; and the pain would continue to get worse.

A few days later, I sat in Coffee Roasters contemplating the whys and hows of this terrible news. As I tried to read Scripture and pray, my mind was preoccupied with what the future would hold. It was such a mix of emotions. Obviously, I was deeply saddened that this was happening to Dale. And yet, there was a small sense of gratitude that God had arranged for Nicole to be so close to her dad during this time.

The next two-and-a-half years of treatment were rough. They tried to attack the disease with radiation and chemotherapy, all of which took a terrible toll on Dale during and after each treatment. There were ongoing trips to a variety of doctors and treatment facilities, mixed with the occasional day of good news. God was sustaining Grandpa longer than the doctors ever gave him. Our second son, Luke, was born during this time. In one of my favorite pictures of Dale, he's holding Luke a few hours after he was born. He was so proud of his grandsons.

Despite seeing the occasional good day, Dale's health was fading slowly but surely. We witnessed Grandpa transform from an active, iconic outdoorsman and Alaskan bush pilot into a broken man who struggled just to get out of his chair. Dale continued to remain strong, and Diane always seemed just a tad stronger. She worked extremely hard trying to stay on top of the tiresome appointments and medication schedules—not to mention the overwhelming paperwork that ensued as she tried to stay current with invoices and insurance companies. She was a truly committed wife and a faithful example of "for better or worse."

WHEN MOURNING BROKE

I was driving back to the hospital where Nicole's dad was being treated when my cell phone started to buzz in my pocket. It was Nicole. She was silent for a few seconds, and then I'll never forget the words that came next. "Dad's gone to be with Jesus now." Within seconds of hearing that single sentence, my stomach twisted. What I was feeling was a very new experience, a terrible one. Sorrowfully, despite all the fighting and hard work, Dale had lost his battle with cancer.

Over the next forty-eight hours, Nicole and I shed more tears than we had ever done before. I had never felt this thing before, and nothing was going to take it away. At three years of age, our little boy, Jude, couldn't quite understand what was going on. He could clearly see and hear the sadness in our home, but he couldn't fully comprehend it. His faith as a child had accepted that Grandpa was now in Heaven and that he would see him again one day. Though Jude was able to accept the loss in his little mind, I was angry and distraught that my boys wouldn't get to experience the fullness of who their grandfather was. Even greater was my frustration in seeing Nicole in so much anguish and being powerless in any ability to remove that pain from her. The famous words of the preacher in Ecclesiastes were never more real than in that moment. It was our "time to weep" and our "time to mourn" (Eccl. 3:4).

A few days later, I wrote the following post:

> It's been a rough week for our family. Early Monday morning, my father-in-law lost his battle with lung cancer. This is my first real, close-to-home experience with grief, and I was not prepared for how debilitating it would be. The first couple days were very difficult, and I found myself full of regret. I wished I had spent less time working and more time with him. There were so many projects that we said we'd complete but never did. I was stricken with sadness over the lack of priority I placed on my time with him. It's now been three days, and the shock has settled a bit. We're trying to focus on getting the memorial service organized for this evening. I don't have much more to say this morning. Thank you to everyone who has been lifting our family up in prayer.

As weeks turned into months, the sense of mourning eased. Of course, it didn't and still doesn't fail to sideswipe us now and again. It might be through a memory fixed within a photo or conversation. All of sudden, we're brought back to Grandpa's bedside, and the pain follows. Even as I wrote the above paragraphs, my eyes welled up with tears as I retold the memory of those days. As time passes, it does become somewhat bittersweet in a way. We know that when Grandpa was a young boy, he gave his life to Jesus in a small Baptist church in Oklahoma. He was often caught reading through the Proverbs, trying to take in Solomon's great wisdom in order to live better, work harder, and care deeper for his family. He was passionate about supporting mission work, assisting in tangible needs being met, and seeing the Gospel being spread throughout foreign people groups. Dale's character and core values provide us with something in which to be joyful. His last days were full of pain and fatigue, but because of his commitment to Christ so many years ago, his suffering was replaced with celebration in Heaven.

This is, perhaps, the good result of mourning. Mourning leaves us with a reminder that our days on earth are numbered. For those of us who know Jesus Christ as our personal Lord and Savior, we will joyfully embrace our eternity in Heaven as Dale did. This being said, until then, we should remain steadfast. We should place our faith at the forefront of everything we say and do. May we experience Christ in a fresh, new way with each new day that we are given breath. May we be bold in our commitment to Christ and our work for Him. Then when we do pass on, the mourning of our friends and family will be met with celebration, both in the good works that we have accomplished and in the life we will now live in Heaven with our Lord.

TAKING TIME TO MOURN

We can never plan for a specific time to mourn. I now believe, though, that we can prepare ourselves on some level. If a loss happens to your friend or acquaintance, it can be of great benefit to clear your schedule for them. There will always be work demands and planned days for recreation. However, loss isn't something we can mark on our calendars. In smaller communities, your employer, coworkers, and friends might even rally around your efforts. We can choose to be prepared, using our gifts and abilities to assist in a time of mourning. On the flipside, if you're the one experiencing the loss of a loved one, it is your time to mourn. Allow the details surrounding burial, memorials, and even the needs of the day to be cared for by the people around you. They will rise to the occasion with their gifts and abilities and surround you in service. Allow that to take place. Trust in their care for you and focus on grieving the one you have lost.

The Body of Christ is brought into powerful unity in times of loss. Petty discussions on ministry plans, budgets, and events get set aside as God's people surround their brothers and sisters. Our role as church leaders is to push everything aside and embrace those moments. Our gifting in leadership can assist us in rallying the people in our local church or maybe even the community, not to mention the enumerable opportunities to share the Gospel with friends and family members who may not know about the saving grace of Jesus Christ. Plan for and assume that at some point in your ministry, you will be taking time to mourn.

CHAPTER ELEVEN

AFRAID OF FALLING
OUT OF LOVE

"May the Lord direct your hearts to the love of God
and to the steadfastness of Christ."

2 Thessalonians 3:5

I was entering into the final year of a three-year religious worker permit serving as youth pastor. The year started with many tangible success markers related to student ministry. We had grown a consistent youth group made up of students from a wide variety of backgrounds. We'd been blessed to see some of them come to faith and be baptized through our ministry. There was a great core team of student and adult leaders. We were well-established in the community for our service projects and facilitated some incredible outreach opportunities.

The icing on the cake was that I had received my religious worker extension from the U.S. government, adding another two years to my term. I suddenly had a clearer vision for the future. I could start thinking about and planning for future ministry goals and objectives. On a personal level, this extension was a huge blessing for Nicole and me and her family. Knowing that we had another couple of years before we had to move back to Canada provided clarity and security.

The first week in February, Nicole and I celebrated the birth of our second son, born on Superbowl Sunday. We actually have a video clip from that day where the TV in the hospital room is on. The Superbowl anthem is playing in the background as we celebrated his arrival. My good friend Scott, who is an NFL fanatic, got a real kick out of that and still does whenever it comes up. That day was absolutely spectacular!

We named our second son Luke Alexander—Luke after the New Testament writer and Alexander after his great-grandfather, Dale's dad. Speaking of Dale, that moment in time, around Luke's birth, was a high point in his cancer treatment as well. Looking at photos of him on that day, you would have never known he was sick. The photos and videos taken of him during those first few weeks of Luke's life became treasured mementos of when we thought he might beat the disease.

THE DOWNWARD SPIRAL—STAGE 1

The year had started with joy, celebration, excitement, and laughter. From the outside looking in, life was amazing for the Norton family. Little did I know, life was about to crumble for Nicole and me. The year that started so well spiraled downward to be filled with sorrow, arguments, fear, anxiety, and uncertainty. Knowing what I know now, the spiral had actually begun a few years previously, related to our finances.

Our personal finances had been in shambles since we moved to Alaska in 2008. Alberta had been booming for almost a decade, and we had capitalized on that boom. We made fifty thousand dollars in eight months buying and selling our first home, a condo apartment. Our second home, an older model townhouse, would make us a mint! That's what I thought, anyway, and convinced Nicole would happen. We took a bit of equity from our previous sale as a down-payment, then took out a huge line of credit to renovate the home. Nicole was skeptical, but I laid out my plan to flip that townhouse, pay off the debt, and have a massive down-payment for our next home.

This plan took a significant plunge downward when we received a letter from the condo association. They required ten thousand dollars from every unit owner for a special assessment to update the doors and windows. Before that moment, I had never heard of a special assessment and couldn't understand how a condo association could make me pay ten grand for new windows and doors—especially when our windows and doors were in good working order. It turns out, these are normal processes outlined in the condo documents to ensure the units all get the same upgrades. This was a new journey for us but a normal journey of owning a condo, so, buyer beware. Enter once again that faithful (or dreadful) line of credit sinking us further into debt.

This next part is so embarrassing but pertinent to understanding the outcome. During those reno days, I had a heavy foot while driving, especially driving down the Deerfoot Trail into Calgary. I was renovating a home, working crazy hours, and going to night school. I racked up a few big tickets and a significant amount of points against my license. Then within a month, I managed to get in two—count them, *two*—car accidents—my own vehicle and then a rental car I was driving while my vehicle was being repaired. Unbelievable, isn't it? Nicole couldn't believe it either! And it gets worse.

The insurance agent advised me that because I had so many points against my license from speeding tickets, I would need to pay for the accidents out of pocket, or my rates would be excruciatingly expensive for the next five years. *Good thing I have that massive line of credit!* I thought. In hindsight, the insurance payments might have cost less in the end because 2008 was just around the corner.

If the year 2008 doesn't ring a bell, it was the year of what is now called the Great Recession. Almost every financial system that we had come to depend on had failed. Industry took a hit, so employment took a hit. Most people were struggling to pay their mortgages, and no one was interested in buying a new home. Within months, the value of our home compared to our mortgage turned upside down. We owed more than it was worth. And don't forget about the line of credit that I had maxed-out because of my careless driving and renovating our now-worthless townhouse. The words of Solomon, though written millennia ago, rang true for us in that moment: "The rich rules over the poor, and the borrower is the slave of the lender" (Prov. 22:7). I had put us into financial slavery, which became the first twist of our downward spiral.

By the grace of God, after I received my call to serve in the North, He provided amazing tenants. They wound up covering all the home expenses during our time in Alaska. That being said, we still rolled up the Alaska Highway dragging a heavy weight of debt. I don't remember the church ever asking about our finances as part of the candidate process, perhaps because at that time, everyone seemed to have money trouble. It has served me well now, though, as I always ask about debt-load whenever anyone is called into full-time ministry. I've lived the difficult—dare I say, crippling—circumstances that it brings.

Coming back to 2011, three years after my arrival, our debt remained. There were moments where we'd make some gains on it. Then a vehicle would break down, or we'd want to take a trip, and the line of credit balance would climb back up. I should have known that this ongoing juggling of personal finances was crushing Nicole. It was weighing down our marriage, but I refused to acknowledge it. I am still in amazement at the grace she showed me and the devotion to our marriage she proved during this journey.

THE DOWNWARD SPIRAL: STAGE 2

Our strained marriage was weighed down even more, and the spiral downward began to pick up speed. The second stage was explained extensively in the previous chapter. That moment of strength and vitality that Nicole's dad experienced after Luke's birth faded quickly. We watched Dale decline over the next five months, and eventually, he passed away on August 1, 2011. This was devastating for Nicole. She had spent so much time with him over the past couple of years. Now, all she wanted was to have him back. As I've already stated, I had never worked through loss and mourning. So, I had also never worked through how long the grieving process could last. For Nicole, working through the passing of her dad was a long, difficult journey. Nicole's grief has taught me that losing a loved one is like a wound that takes a long time to heal, a wound that tends to open back up frequently before it ever fully scars over. And even then, there always remains some residual ache and numbness that never fully goes away.

All the while, we were raising a three-year-old and a newborn, which was a blessing but added to the stress and workload of life. I was spending a lot of time at the church and in the community, which meant Nicole was solo-parenting more than she should have ever had to. Especially during that time! To my embarrassment, I likely spent far too much time working during those days. I should have explained the household heartache we were experiencing to our leadership and maybe taken some time off to spend with her and the boys. I just didn't know enough, or perhaps I ignored what the Spirit was revealing to me. I should have been better, done better.

THE DOWNWARD SPIRAL: STAGE 3

At the same time, believe it or not, our church was falling apart. There were struggles between the elders and our lead pastor about work hours, finances, preaching content and quality, and differences of opinion on ministry philosophy. There was no big moral failure or single issue fallout, just the burden of leadership, losing missional focus, and not getting along. As is often the case in these types of leadership struggles, certain members of the congregation become aware and get involved. Factions began to be established, while most of the congregation was oblivious to what was taking place behind closed doors.

As youth pastor, I sat in on most of the meetings and took part as best I could. As a first-time pastor, I let myself get wrapped up in the whole situation to a very unhealthy level. Looking back, I have a lot more clarity on the situation and the road that we all journeyed. I see that it could have been prevented on numerous occasions. I also see that my insecurities and inexperience definitely added to the problems. This is my greatest regret in all my ministry time spent in Alaska—that I was not a voice pointing to our mission and vision. I got wrapped up in the opinions and politics and missed so many opportunities to bring peace and unity into the conflicts. Instead, I believe I added to the conflict with unhelpful comments and concerns.

Eventually, Pastor Keith resigned, and some were satisfied with his decision. Others were devastated. And we all learned a valuable lesson about *most* of the congregation. Remember how I said they were oblivious? This is how we found out. During a church meeting after Keith's resignation, we listened to people stand and give account on the amazing ministry that Keith had brought into their personal lives and our church. They felt completely blindsided. Losing their pastor wounded them deeply.

This was solidified after Keith and his family started attending another local church to heal. In the next few months, we watched a third of our congregation move over to that church—not because Keith was preaching, but in silent support of him. They chose to leave to simply be near him, to make a statement about the ministry he had for them in years past. This taught me a valuable lesson. I learned that most of a pastor's ministry goes unnoticed. It doesn't happen in the nine-to-five workday; it happens through phone calls and text messages, emails and social media posts. Most of all, it happens through handshakes and hugs, during times of celebration and sorrow that happen weekly but that never make it into any sort of report.

Before I move on to the final stage of my downward spiral, I need to be clear that I currently have good relationships with all parties involved. Time and distance tend to heal, and hindsight often brings clarity. Moreover, God is faithful and merciful. "The steadfast love of the LORD never ceases; his mercies never come to an end; they are new every morning; great is your faithfulness. 'The LORD is my portion,' says my soul, 'therefore I will hope in him'" (Lam. 3:22-24). I think everyone involved during that difficult time wishes we had communicated differently, been more patient and gracious, and sought out other options for reconciliation. We all learned a *lot* during that season of ministry. Although it caused great pain and disruption for our church, and even for our local community, I believe God redeemed much of it, helping us all become better spiritual leaders.

THE FINAL STAGE AND NEW HOPE

I didn't realize how much not having Pastor Keith around would impact my life. Being a youth pastor without a senior pastor to seek support for ministry plans and projects was difficult. As an extrovert, I'm a verbal processor, and I needed someone of whom to bounce off ideas. The elders truly tried their best, but it wasn't the same. Each elder often had different thoughts and responses. Each elder viewed me differently. Each perceived my perspectives with different value and intent. This was a very stressful time, and I continued to spiral downward, making poor decisions often based in emotion.

Then I started to bring the confusion I was feeling at the church into our home. I couldn't stop thinking about and talking about our church that seemed to be falling apart. This increased the overall negativity that already hung over Nicole and me. Our marriage was really suffering.

Before that time, I had never understood how couples in ministry could end up divorced. I had always viewed them as such rock-solid people with rock-solid marriages. Now I realize that most people likely thought that of Nicole and me because so much is hidden from the church and community. And yet in that moment in 2011, I remember thinking for the first time, *This is how it happens; this is how pastors end up divorced.* It wasn't long after that thought came to mind, and likely after a long argument, that I said to Nicole, "We need help." She agreed.

Believe it or not, we actually lived next door to a Christian counseling center called New Hope Counseling. It was connected to Alaska Christian

College, a local Bible college that also owned the property on which we lived. Even though I never worked for the Bible college, they were gracious to provide affordable housing for us as a ministry family. I had pretty good relationships with both Keith, the college president (not to be confused with Pastor Keith), and his wife Debbie, who facilitated the counseling practice. Keith and Debbie had attended our church, and their son attended our youth group.

As I write this, the irony is like a slap in the face. I should have walked over there months before. I can only assume that the same pride and arrogance that brought about so many of my struggles also kept me from booking an appointment before that moment. I have come to realize that many times in life, God has often provided people and resources that we can't see because of sin or sorrow. If we could only pause in the storm of heartache and ask the Spirit to help us see, we might find that help is as close as next door!

So, I walked over there and asked for help. I told them that Nicole and I needed marriage counseling. In the beginning, I assumed that we would meet with Keith and Debbie as a couple—or at least with Debbie, since we had decent relationships with them. That being said, perhaps for this reason, it was wise of Debbie to refer us to another counselor in the practice. That's when I was introduced to Peggy.

Before the initial visit, Nicole and I were each asked to fill out the same intake form, answering a wide variety of questions about the struggles we were having, including questions about our thoughts and feelings about those struggles. We each submitted the forms separately, not knowing what each other had written. Heading to the first appointment was internally tumultuous. Nicole and I both had knots in our stomachs, and I think Peggy could tell. She told us to take a deep breath and that Nicole and I were in a good place—not only because we had decided to seek out counseling, but also because our intake forms provided evidence that we were going to pull through. The final question on the form was, "In your own words, state the concerns that bring you to counseling." Our answers were almost exact: we were "afraid of falling out of love."

Hearing that Nicole felt the same way gave me a new hope (pun intended). Our communication had broken down months before, and yet there it was, a statement that included two significant assumptions. Being "afraid of falling out of love" meant that we both were still *in* love and wanted to *remain* in love. Peggy could see that this statement was healing to us. She acknowledged that we had experienced and were experiencing significant life-change in a number of areas, leading to pressure that has impacted our marriage. She explained that any couple could be experiencing difficulties if they were working through one or two of the half-dozen items with which we were dealing.

Peggy started to outline each of them, tapping her fingers as she relayed back to us the information we had given her. We were in debt; we had lost a parent; we had our second child; we had a property back home that was worth less than we owed; our church was in turmoil; my career was uncertain, which meant our immigration status was uncertain. This, of course, didn't include the family history dynamics and communication breakdowns that we brought into the mix, adding to the overall weight we were feeling as a couple. Inadvertently, somehow, the pain, anxiety, and frustration of these individual struggles transferred to our marriage. Peggy showed us that although we could not immediately change or remove these big life events that we were facing, we could choose to face them together. We could choose to submit to God what we couldn't control and choose to work together on what we could control. She centered us back on Jesus, then each other.

We walked away from that first appointment filled with hope. I remember being shocked that a single appointment had made such a significant impact on me. I really felt a renewed closeness to Nicole, like we had been realigned as a couple. But please don't hear these words as a quick-fix statement. Peggy gave us hope, but she also gave us homework. We worked through *His Needs,*

Her Needs by Dr. Willard F. Harley (an excellent book that I now suggest to every couple asking for marital resources.) Over the coming months, we met with Peggy every couple of weeks, outlining what we had worked on and touching on how those big life events were impacting us. Slowly but surely, Nicole and I started having more productive conversations, and we started praying together more. This moved us both into a state of openness and willingness to change, allowing the Holy Spirit's convicting and encouraging work to carry us along.

BEING AFRAID

Looking back, I often think about that first appointment and those words "afraid of falling out of love." Being afraid was a good thing in that moment. Other than my relationship with Christ, my marriage is the most valuable relationship I will ever have. By being afraid of losing it, there was a preventative quality that sunk in, causing me to accept the current state of my marriage and walk my feet over to that counseling center. Being afraid helped me make the right decision.

Perhaps this is why being afraid, in itself, is not directly associated with evil. Instead, being afraid is contextual, not always stemming from a sin issue. Sure, there is a fear of getting caught when we have done something wrong. The Holy Spirit's conviction aids us in these moments, helping us see the value of confession of that sin and submission to the consequences. Conversely, fear can keep us from those consequences that carry a sting worth preventing. In its basic human form, fear can keep us from danger. We who live in the North have a very healthy fear of the environment, the wilderness, and the predators who roam the landscape. Fear can't prevent us from making poor decisions that could lead to harm or even death.

What about being afraid of God? Scripture is clear that spiritually, fearing the Lord is a healthy place to be. Solomon stated, "Blessed is the one who fears the LORD always" (Prov. 28:14). Isaiah, prophesying from the Lord, wrote, "This is the one to whom I will look: he who is humble and contrite in spirit and trembles at my word" (Isa. 66:2). Paul called the early church to "work out your own salvation with fear and trembling, for it is God who works in you, both to will and to work for his good pleasure" (Phil. 2:12-13). When I read about Jesus' prayer to His Father on the Mount of Olives before His arrest and pending execution, I believe our Savior was experiencing fear (Luke 22:39-44). Through His fear and anguish, sweating like flowing blood, I am overwhelmed with thanksgiving that He willing embraced what we could never endure.

What would it look like if we decidedly leaned into being afraid when it arose in our hearts? Not fully giving into it, but focusing in on it as a starting point, inviting the Spirit's insight into that moment. Asking ourselves, is this fear rational? Is this fear preventing us from danger or a poor decision? Is this fear preventing us from sin? Is this fear revealing something of value and importance, something that would be devastating to lose? Leaning into being afraid might just bring us further clarity into God's desire for us in that moment and maybe even His will for our future. We may find ourselves willing to submit to His will and, if needed, cry out for help and counsel, bringing about healing and restoration.

CHAPTER TWELVE

A PREFERENCE PANDEMIC

"Rejoice in hope, be patient in tribulation, be constant in prayer.
Contribute to the needs of the saints and seek to show hospitality."

Romans 12:12-13

Sometimes, I think back to my days before my ministry in the North. I worked sales in the hospitality industry, selling corporate meeting packages. I worked in Calgary, and the economy was booming during that time. Although there was a lot of business to go around, as a sales team, we were constantly trying to get an edge on the competition. We'd look for tips on new project meetings or events, trying to lock in clients before they even started looking for a location. The goal was to book the function before another hotel even knew it was happening; before anyone else could get a quote into the client's hands. Alternatively, if we heard of a function happening with another hotel chain, we tried to out-quote them and swing the business our way. We were constantly trying to get an edge on the competition.

Booking a client is just the beginning of the competition. The communication and preparation leading up to the event can increase the chance for future wins. They prefer email, you email. They prefer a text, you text. They want to spend twenty minutes on the phone telling you about their daughter's graduation, you listen. They want to stop by the venue multiple times to get a picture of what the event might look like, you book it into your schedule. Because it's not just about *that* event. Repeat business is crucial to the sales game; it is absolutely the easiest way to stay ahead of the competition when the client comes back time and time again without ever looking elsewhere. Most of the time, the client will keep coming back because they know the cost and what to expect, but most of all, they know you. And that previous relationship can make all the difference.

After my career-shift into ministry, I went in assuming that every church worked together. If the end goal was spreading the Gospel and making disciples, why wouldn't churches work together at all times and in all capacities? Sunday morning couldn't matter that much, could it? If one church building's full, wouldn't you just send them to another one? I was so naive to how Western church structure worked and how church leaders had been thrust into a competition in the ministry world that mirrored my previous career in hospitality sales. Moreover, living in the North gave me a microcosm perspective of this observation. Consider the limited resources and fixed population. Filling a church building on Sunday morning is typically a marker of success but a significant challenge in the North. Excluding choosing a church based on the theological reasons, which is completely valid by the way, I quickly learned that there are a lot of ways churches compete for *business*. (Am I allowed to say that?)

THE COMPETITIVE WESTERN CHURCH

Much like choosing a hotel for an event or function, choosing a church has become centered around preferences. Yes, I said preferences. I think this is where a lot of our competition stems from—preferences in the venue itself, the type of services that are offered, and the level of customer service provided by those who serve, direct, communicate, and lead. A pastor for example, can be doctrinally on-point with engaging preaching and teaching, yet someone might change churches based on his mannerisms or personality. I know at the onset; this might sound crazy. But I also know this exists because I was a part of it before I was in ministry. I didn't realize it at the time, but now that

I serve and lead in the church, my eyes have been opened. I was an adherent to the preference competition that exists in the Western church. Although Nicole and I were always faithful church members—and for the most part, we chose churches based on theology—we also chose churches (the building and the people in them) that fit our preferences. There were certain styles of music, dress code, and preaching dynamics that we preferred. And I know we're not the only ones. In fact, most of the church attenders that I've known adhere to their preferences as well.

I remember listening to pastor and author Francis Chan speak at a conference, giving an account from his missionary work in Asia. He was building a network of contacts within the underground church. Pastors and church leaders would ask him to explain what church was like in the West. At one point, Francis told them that Westerners would often travel farther distances, past other church buildings, to attend a particular church that holds their preferred music style or children's program. The people listening to the account began to laugh, thinking he was telling them a joke. Francis told them he wasn't joking, trying to explain why people would make these choices. They continued to laugh. He had to give up and move on to another topic of conversation. These people who risk their lives to be a part of the Church could not wrap their heads around competing preferences between church buildings.

Obviously, the goal of this account was to give us a reality check, which it definitely did. We had all received Chan's message, and it resonated with us. Nevertheless, at the end of the conference, we all still returned to our competing, preference-based, Western churches, existing in our competing, preference-based, Western culture. We still had no idea how to change the minds of the average Western church attender. Although it didn't feel right, we couldn't directly call out any one individual stating that they were wrong or sinful because it all stemmed from Western culture as a whole. As I've tried to get to the bottom of this never-ending rabbit hole, I've had to come to grips with the possibility that serving in the competitive Western church might be part of my calling.

Now, before I get theological pushback—or worse, get called a heretic—allow me to expand on this topic a bit further, entering into the spiritual realm for a moment. Despite our Western propensity to choose a church based on preference, I absolutely believe that the Holy Spirit may lead an individual to a specific church community, during a specific time, for a specific purpose. "Likewise the Spirit helps us in our weakness . . . the Spirit intercedes for the saints according to the will of God" (Rom. 8:26-27). Sometimes, the Spirit can and will lead someone to a church community that is completely outside of their preferences, often in hindsight, for a specific work to be completed within the Lord's greater Gospel plan. However, I cannot ignore that in my experience, for whatever reason inside God's sovereignty, this is not the norm.

Don't believe me? If you live in the West, start taking a poll in your community context. Speak to your community's pastors, ministers, and church leaders. I'm certain they will validate that an attender's choice in church is most often connected with their preferences. How do they know? They're the ones hearing the reasons people arrive, the reasons people stay, and the reasons people move on to the next church. As church leaders try to assess these circumstances, they struggle to find a balance. On one hand, we're nervous that we might be simply adhering to their preferences in order to keep them in the seats. On the other hand, we might be legitimately "contribut[ing] to the needs of the saints and seek[ing] to show hospitality" (Rom. 12:13). Within this struggle, the competition creeps in. Soon enough, church leaders are trying to get an edge on what the majority of people are looking for in a church, hopefully without ever laying down their theology. The competition ensues, even though no one really wants it, but as church leaders, we have to admit it exists. We've learned to package this Western church reality within the term *ministry philosophy* because it communicates our purposes a lot better than the word *competition*. This term also speaks to our heart condition, that we want to find a balance. We want to serve the people who enter into our doors, but we don't want to perpetuate the problem. Like I said, it's a struggle.

NORTHERN CHURCH COMPETITION

The North is not immune to the realities of competing, preference-based church. In fact, remember that I said Northern ministry becomes a microcosm of this cultural moment. I would add that smaller Northern communities can have a greater struggle in this regard. Allow me to explain why. Both on the Kenai Peninsula of Alaska where I started my ministry career and in Whitehorse, Yukon, where I serve now, it feels like there's a church on every corner. It seems like every denomination, fellowship, and network has an outpost in these Northern communities. This cultural identifier has a mix of pros and cons. One pro to having a variety of churches is that it provides lots of options. For those wishing to attend a church, they can choose the option that fits their preferences. Yup, there's that word again! Church-goers can choose their theology or ministry philosophy, music or preaching styles, children or youth programs, or hop between a few options. Not that I think hopping between churches is a beneficial idea. I'm simply noting that it's an option that, whether we like it or not, some people take. And remember that I said it was a *pro* for the average church attender, but it's also connected to our *con*.

The con to having a lot of churches in a Northern community relates to the struggle for consistent attendance and, therefore, consistent resources in both finances and volunteerism. Every church community needs a certain number of dedicated members to serve and finance the ministries, including the hiring of staff to direct events and programs. Depending on the options provided, there's a struggle to obtain that critical mass. Western church-growth barriers typically begin at fifty regular attenders; then two hundred becomes the next ceiling. At fifty attenders, there is usually only enough donations to maintain a single full-time salary for a pastor or minister. That being said, having so many churches in such a lightly populated area, the numbers can vary greatly from one local church to another. I've come to learn that in Northern communities, this is the reality. Many local churches are simply too small to hire more staff than a solo pastor, some of them only affording a part-time pastor.

Take the Yukon, for example. The capital city of Whitehorse holds three-fourths of the territory's forty-thousand-resident population. If Whitehorse churches struggle to consistently support their pastoral leaders, imagine how hard it is for the outlying communities. The result? It's impossible to support even a part-time pastor or minister without having significant missions support from outside churches located in large urban centers. And some of them never receive this option. Their church reality is to receive a single church service, once a month, from a single denomination or fellowship by a visiting pastor, minister, or priest. In this situation, the choice often does become theological and not preferential. The few church attenders in that community become segregated into camps, choosing to associate with an outside church through online gatherings or watching whatever televangelist that comes with their cable package.

CHURCH PREFERENCE VS. GOSPEL PREVENTION

Some of you have been reading this chapter and are dying inside. You've been saying to yourself, "Who cares about the preferences of people inside the church? Why don't you focus on reaching the people outside the church? Why not focus on spreading the Gospel?" If that's your take, I love it! I'm right there with you. Most of these church competitions are based on the preferences of church-going people, who have an established idea of what they want—an idea that is often dated when compared to culture. If we're not careful, adhering to the preference of a churched person may become the prevention of reaching an unchurched person with the Gospel. After all, we must keep the mission in the forefront of everything we do that we may continue being "a light" to "bring salvation to the ends of the earth" (Act. 13:47).

Northern ministry has helped me understand this significantly. Other than maybe the Bible Belt of the United States, the West has moved toward a post-Christian culture. Northern Canada is a frontrunner to this shift. Speaking to my current context, Statistics Canada reports that fifty percent of Yukoners are atheist or agnostic.[2] Then add in other faith positions. Then add in the complex religious history of Indigenous Peoples in the North, with the realities of church and government programs that had a variety of devastating outcomes. My pastoral ministry in the North has given me a glimpse into the future of the entire Western world. No longer can we assume that people know or understand anything founded in Christian tradition or culture.

Gone are the days where the majority of Western people attended church on Sunday morning. When a church leader transitions a congregation's focus away from churched preference, they actually begin a shift toward a larger group of people. Soon, that congregation is building relationships with unchurched people, and their preference-based bias loses its luster. Long-standing traditions become optional as Gospel-driven ministry becomes the primary focus in day-to-day church life. Furthermore, in extreme cases, theology shifts, bringing to light false doctrines as hearts are softened and a burden for the lost is unfolded and captured.

COVID COMPETITION

Church competition couldn't have been witnessed in a greater capacity than during the COVID-19 pandemic, when church moved from in-house to online gatherings. At first, in March 2020, there was an upward swing for any and all churches that moved to online attendance. Times were uncertain, and people were scared, so they sought out spiritual insight. In those first

2   "Yukon (Code 60) (table), National Household Survey (NHS) Profile, 2011 National Household Survey, Catalogue no. 99-004-XWE," Statistics Canada, Released September 11, 2013, http://www12.statcan.gc.ca/nhs-enm/2011/dp-pd/prof/index.cfm?Lang=E.

few weeks, hosting church online was a scramble. Mobile phones were rigged up with terrible audio, but people showed up. I remember Pastor Ed Wiley tweeting out this prayer request the week before Easter: "Pray for pastors as they attempt to make this Sunday's livestream not look like a bin Laden capture video."[3] Despite the humor, it was a valid prayer request. And it was retweeted over a million times!

The increase in online attendance lasted through to digital Easter. Then online attendance began to decline for most churches. Over the next couple of months, big budgets and production paid off. Larger, innovative churches thrived during the pandemic. Smaller, traditional churches struggled to survive. And many didn't make it. I remember hearing stats from groups like *Barna* and *LifeWay* pointing to it.[4] [5] Pastors from across the Western world were struggling with it. I even heard Northern church attenders admitting to it. The dynamics of larger church productions made for a more targeted viewing experience. Attenders of the competing, preference-based church were now able to simply swipe up on a mobile device if they wanted another option. And that's what they did.

For example, imagine you're in a worship gathering of fifty people, and the back-up vocalist is getting really pitchy in the middle of the second worship song. We realize that her singing has become a distraction. In that moment, we could never conceive the idea of a dozen of those fifty people suddenly getting up in the middle of that worship song and heading out the door. It just wouldn't happen. No matter how pitchy the singer got, we'd all stay in our seats. Why? Perhaps out of guilt or conviction to respect the person singing or the simple embarrassment of people watching us walk

---

3   Ed Wiley, Twitter Post, March 19, 2020, 10:22 AM. https://twitter.com/EdWiley/status/1240690108807778304.

4   David Kinnaman, "One in Three Practicing Christians Has Stopped Attending Church During COVID-19," Barna.com,, July 8, 2020, https://www.barna.com/research/new-sunday-morning-part-2.

5   Aaron Earls, "5 COVID-19 Problems That Worsened for Pastors This Summer," LifewayResearch.com, August 7, 2020, https://lifewayresearch.com/2020/08/07/5-covid-19-problems-that-worsened-for-pastors-this-summer.

out. Now, shift to the pandemic online worship gathering. Post digital Easter metrics showed us that a viewing of fifty people could easily drop by a dozen viewers with any error in performance or even a momentary audio or video glitch. Those twelve people had no problem swiping to the next feed instead of enduring that pitchy audio because no one's watching them. And when no one's watching, there is no accountability preventing our Western preference-based mindset to win out. We don't even think about it; we simply react, choosing what we prefer based on what's available. And there is a *lot* of available options!

PHYSICAL CHURCH VS. DIGITAL CHURCH

Some of you are dying to push back. I get it; the Church is not a building. And the Church isn't an online feed either. Let's dig into that a bit. During the COVID lockdowns, large churches learned to produce a very personal viewing experience with multiple interactive components throughout the service and numerous opportunities to connect during the feed and after the online gathering had concluded. For me, this was significant proof that the Church is the people. People stayed on the feed longer and tuned back in more frequently when the experience was centered in on helping people feel connected during a time when we were forced to separate. For smaller churches with minimal tech and a static smartphone experience, it was simply not engaging on a personal level.

Reading that hurts a bit, doesn't it? I know it hurts because I've felt it! For those of us living in smaller communities, serving smaller churches, the pandemic brought us to the brink of self-destruction. We tried so hard to compete with the larger churches and their dynamic, viewer-friendly worship experiences. We didn't have enough time. We didn't have enough money. We didn't have enough people. We didn't have enough energy. We didn't have enough capacity. And we felt like failures as those viewing numbers declined week after week. Maybe you had church attenders who openly admitted to you, "We wanted to let you know that our family has moved to _____ Church. We're sorry, but it's just a better viewing experience." Although I understood their intensions were good and they were simply trying to be honest with what they had decided, it still stings to hear it.

Then there was the battle of physical versus digital church. What a divisive nightmare! On one hand, we were thankful for those attenders who remained faithful week in and week out. On the other hand, many of them drained us, bombarding us with opinions on the pros and cons of whichever encampment they chose to align. As if the lockdowns weren't stressful enough, reopening became the pinnacle of the preference competition. Each camp constantly pulled the church leader's ear with assumptive statements and suggestive demands on leadership approach and decisions that should be made. The decline in attendance, matched with the division within those who remained, became overwhelming. Many small to mid-sized church pastors and ministers, regretfully including myself, burned out four to six months into the pandemic. The competing, preference-based church consumed us.

Thankfully, every pastor I spoke to over those months stated that they always had a core of faithful viewers who tuned in every week. Regardless of the quality of the digital experience, including tech difficulties, they were committed to tune in each week. Even after digital Easter, when online attendance took a significant decline through May and June 2020, these committed members and attenders were a lifeline for many pastors of smaller to mid-sized churches. For those attenders—you know who you are—I offer my thanks on behalf of every pastor and minister who served through the pandemic.

THE PAST AND THE FUTURE

In reflection, I believe the COVID-19 pandemic simply amplified what was already happening in Western society for decades prior. Whether you live in the American Bible Belt or Canada's Northern Territories, digital church proved that church competition is alive and well and not going to change anytime soon. People have their preferences, even Christians. Or maybe I should say, especially Christians? If preferences are not being met, we go searching for another option. The pandemic gave every church attender permission to try other churches in anonymity. Even many of those who remained faithful refused to be encamped in divisive positions and chose to support their pastors and ministers still took in other online worship gatherings. And why not, since there are hundreds of thousands of options from which they can choose?

That being said, I'd like to end by considering the global outcome. I suspect that the pandemic will have spread this Western mindset across the world. With the globalization of internet access and a global propensity to look westward for the latest and greatest, it's not hard to believe. The global Church may face its very first preference pandemic. This, of course, will only last if Christianity continues to experience freedom. In countries where the Church can worship without fear of persecution, people will be able to choose where and how they want to experience church gatherings.

Conversely, there will always be those in the Church who are underground, facing persecution. Those whom Francis Chan met with and spoke about at the conference I attended. They have no options for competing, preference-based church attendance. In a society and culture where Scripture is illegal and open worship is outlawed, any physical or digital gathering of the saints is like Heaven on earth. If I'm to be honest with myself, I whisper a hesitant prayer for this to be brought to the Western world—selfishly, so that I can escape the competition and sacrificially, so that the Gospel may spread.

That, however, is not my current calling. For reasons that I can only submit to God's sovereign will, I have been called to reach and serve a Northern, Western culture. In my cultural moment, independence and self-expression are idolized as the way to live and thrive. I live in a comfortable, predominantly atheist-agnostic culture, where half of the people who live in my community reject the idea of God or have no care to find out if God exists. Almost everyone I interact with, inside or outside the church, is comfortable within the never-ending options and distractions of life. This is my community. This is my context. This is my calling. If you're serving in the Western world like I am, you're likely facing similar cultural realities and competition and the same preference-based church dynamics that I've outlined in this chapter. Whether we like it or not, this is our moment. May we submit into God's sovereign hands what we cannot change about this current cultural reality. And as we journey through it, may we continue embracing creativity and innovation, allowing the Spirit's leading toward new opportunities to share the Gospel. Lord willing, we will reach new attenders and viewers, pressing on with our hope solely in Christ that they might hear the Gospel and be brought into His Church.

KNOW YOUR CALLING

There have been many books and resources written on how to create effective ministry within the local church. These materials have aided numerous pastors and ministry leaders, present company included. There's just one problem. Almost all of them seem to make the assumption that ministry is lived out within a large, urban context or at least a mid-sized city. Of course, this doesn't stop us from using them. We give it our best shot. We work tirelessly, trying to bring these models into our compact communities. As plans are implemented, they don't adequately fulfil what is needed in our smaller contexts. Realistically, they don't often fit the thousands of small to mid-sized churches found all over the Western world, including most of the churches found in big cities. This is because there are different challenges that we face in doing ministry in our smaller communities. They create a compact environment for life and ministry that cause every action to have an immediate and, quite often, personal reaction.

No, this isn't a final word written against mega churches or even large churches. I believe church methods and models should be as unique as the Christians found inside of them. There's plenty of room under the grace of the Gospel for all sizes and types of church. We should all keep trying new things and sharing the wealth of ideas. This is why I don't want anyone to be mistaken in thinking that the thoughts and lessons shared in this book are the be-all and end-all ministry guidelines. I am simply sending my Northern community perspective out to the world with the hope that it might help someone, somewhere, on their ministry journey. I submit to you that my perspective is not better, just different.

Where are you right now? As you finish this book, where do you physically live and serve? Are you in a rural town surrounded by farmland? Are you in a quaint seaside port? Perhaps you're in an isolated context. A forested hamlet in the mountains. A Northern wilderness village. Perhaps you're the small community within the larger one—on the outside as a commuter-driven bedroom municipality, on the inside as a trendy downtown neighborhood. What type of community are you in right now? Wherever you are, God has given you that place, on this day, for a specific reason. Therefore, your community needs *you*. This is your calling. My prayer is that God will show you that with the right vision and the right team, matched with a fervent dependency on His leading, successful ministry is possible in your community. Regardless of its size or location, you can—and will—experience incredible wins! Ultimately, that's what we're all striving for, right? Gospel-driven Kingdom wins?

To anyone who might be struggling to provide a solid ministry within your community, take heart. I understand that you might not have a three hundred-plus congregation from which to pull your resources. I know what it's like to have a handful of people make up your leadership team and most, if not all, of them volunteers. Maybe you're without a lead pastor, or your local body has gone through a time of "transition." (Now, there's a loaded church-term.) I've been there, too. Maybe you're being pulled apart by divisive encampments, and you're trying to find the centerline. Maybe you've lost some great people to another church or ministry, or maybe they've walked away from the faith. These are painful trials that every pastor knows. Lastly, and maybe the most difficult to hear, perhaps you've allowed some personal opinion or unresolved sin destroy some of what God has provided. Don't give up! We've all been there. I'll say it again, take heart.

Despite all these hurdles, I've learned some valuable lessons. I've experienced the growth that Christ can provide by leaning into Him for strength and identity, while serving alongside a dedicated, multi-generational, grassroots team. Remain steadfast and unified with Him and with your team. The road may be rocky and full of obstacles. Nevertheless, you have everything you need to experience and achieve the life-changing ministry for which your heart is yearning. Remember that any ministry, even those in smaller communities, can have a massive Kingdom impact. Be encouraged and "press on toward the goal for the prize of the upward call of God in Christ Jesus" (Phil. 3:14). Trust that there is no hurdle or trial that will prevent the Holy Spirit's conviction and calling nor prevent the saving grace of our Lord Jesus Christ. As pastors, ministers, and church leaders, may we all trust in our calling toward that truth.

ABOUT THE AUTHOR

Jeremy is the lead pastor of Mountainview Church in Whitehorse, Yukon Territory, Canada. He strives to facilitate his life and ministry around his personal mission, "To serve Christ by cultivating biblical leadership through writing, equipping, and communications."

A NOTE FROM THE AUTHOR

I have not taken the most direct career path to get me where I am today. Both in education and experience, I have moved in and out of the business and ministry worlds. I don't believe this happened by mistake. God has clearly meshed these two career paths to provide me with some valuable insight into reaching others. Currently, my role as lead pastor provides numerous opportunities for preaching, teaching, networking, and leading in a variety of capacities.

Connecting with other people energizes me, be it face-to-face, online, or through social media. I'm a podcast and audio book junky, based more in non-fiction genres with leadership content or "How-to" themes. I like anything made by Apple and find myself dabbling in photo and video editing from time to time.

When the tech side of my brain needs a break, I'm an average guitar player and vocalist and have always been involved in music and church worship teams. I thoroughly enjoy worship music, although my iTunes playlists carry a wide variety of genres.

Spending time in God's creation also refreshes me, so I try to engage in a wide variety of outdoor pursuits, depending on the season. And no matter what I'm doing, coffee is a staple. From high-priced espresso to gas-station joe, I've tried it all, and I'm just happy to get a cup.

Lastly and most importantly, I cherish my time with my wife, Nicole, and our three boys, Jude, Luke, and Mark. Some days, nothing's better than a family movie night with all five of us snuggled into one bed with a big bowl of popcorn. Although I don't always get it right, I try to remind myself daily that biblical leadership begins at home!

I enjoy writing. From sermons, to blog posts, to content for online articles, or book projects, writing is a key piece to God's calling on my life. Much of the content found within this book originated on my site, LeadBiblically.com. I strive to write at least once each week, providing thought-provoking articles, ministry resources, and leadership training tips. Most content stems from a Christian worldview, containing numerous biblical references. Furthermore, you'll find a fair share of personal life experience as I strive to become the leader God has called me to be.

To receive my latest posts, I suggest subscribing via email, which you can do right now from the Lead Biblically landing page. Or feel free to use the search tool, also located on the landing page. Alternately, check my Archives Page and scroll through a variety of posts and resources that may be of interest to you. If all that seems like a bit too much work, I'd suggest starting with the most popular Lead Biblically posts, chosen by readers just like you:

- Three Qualities That Made Joshua a Great Leader
- Long Gone to the Yukon
- Providing a Simple Definition for Outreach

CONTACT INFORMATION

Whether you're interested in leadership, writing, equipping, or communications, it's time to connect! Please feel free to contact me via email at jeremy@leadbiblically.com or on my cell at 867-335-7524. I'm looking forward to connecting with you in the future! For local contacts, I'd be more than willing to meet and grab a coffee. To fellow authors, I'm always looking for new resources. If the fit is right, I'd welcome your content as a potential guest post for my blog. For Skype or FaceTime users, drop me a message to set up a video call. For any social media junkies like myself, choose your preferred network:

- Twitter: PastorJNorton
- Facebook.com/PastorJeremyNorton
- Instagram.com/PastorJeremyNorton

Thanks for joining me on this journey, serving Christ by cultivating biblical leadership!

In His Service,

Jeremy

Ambassador International's mission is to magnify the Lord Jesus Christ and promote His Gospel through the written word.

We believe through the publication of Christian literature, Jesus Christ and His Word will be exalted, believers will be strengthened in their walk with Him, and the lost will be directed to Jesus Christ as the only way of salvation.

For more information about
AMBASSADOR INTERNATIONAL
please visit:

www.ambassador-international.com
@AmbassadorIntl
www.facebook.com/AmbassadorIntl

Thank you for reading this book. Please consider leaving us a review on your social media, favorite retailer's website, Goodreads or Bookbub, or our website.

More from Ambassador International

Through vignettes of fresh water springs and fly fishing analogies, *Theology From the Spring* provides the reader with eyes for seeing how God's creation— the natural world—can provide answers to the oldest divine mystery and make sense of the beauty and chaos we see within the created order.

Join Christine Paxson and Rose Spiller as they explore the answers to these and many other questions about the true Gospel message in *No Half-Truths Allowed: Understanding the Complete Gospel Message.* Learn what Jesus did for you, why He did it, and how you can articulate the Gospel to others.

In *Transformed Thinking*, Tom Wheeler clearly lays out the most fundamental beliefs of Christianity and compares them to other worldviews, providing arguments to support his beliefs. Even though this book is purposed for the classroom setting, it would be a beneficial read for any believer who wants to have a firm foundation on which to share their beliefs with unbelievers.

Printed in the USA
CPSIA information can be obtained
at www.ICGtesting.com
LVHW022311170923
758471LV00026B/453